INFORMATION TECHNOLOGY IN 21ST CENTURY

INFORMATION TECHNOLOGY IN 21ST CENTURY

(In 9 Volumes)

ETHICS AND GOVERNANCE OF THE INTERNET

(Volume 4)

PROF. RAMESH CHANDRA

Vice-Chancellor, Bundelkhand University, Jhansi (U.P.)

Publication

KALPAZ PUBLICATIONS

DELHI–110052

INFORMATION TECHNOLOGY IN 21ST CENTURY
Ethics and Governance of the Internet
(Information Technolgy)

Rs. 8000 (Set)
Rs. 900 (each volume)

ISBN: 81-7835-158-7 (Set)
ISBN: 81-7835-162-5 (Vol. 4)

Published in 2003 in India by
Kalpaz Publications
C-30, Satyawati Nagar
Delhi-110052
E-mail: kalpaz@hotmail.com

Laser Typesetting at: A.S. Printers
Printed at: Chawla Offset Printers, Delhi

Preface

In this wired-up era, the inhabitants of the knowledge societies will have all the more freedom, flexibility and opportunities to decide how they would like to be governed and by whom. The underlying truth will become self-evident that it is not the leaders who govern people but it is the people who let the leaders govern them. It is a well-acknowledged fact that access to information plays a critical role in setting up of governance/control mechanisms. This process is founded on extraction and accumulation of information and using it to the effect which creates hierarchical structures on which power gets unequally distributed.

The information technologies can influence the process of governance in various ways and in varying degrees, from improving the current mechanisms of delivery of services to transforming the entire mechanism and the nature of services themselves. Digital governance is a popular term to focus on the new, evolving forms of governance—electronic governance. Good governance rests on the pillars of knowledge and recognition of this set of knowledge by the decision-makers. Digitisation of this entire set of knowledge within a network which links every individual including the decision-makers and gives democratic freedom to everyone to access and make use of this knowledge paves the way for digital governance.

Introduction of internet governance is a way to ensure that common citizens have equal right to be a part of decision-making processes which affect them directly or indirectly, and influence them in a manner which best improves their conditions and the quality of lives. The new form of governance will ensure that citizens are no longer passive consumers of services offered to them and would transform them to play a decisive role in deciding the kind of services they want and the structure which could best provide the same.

This book is an academic exercise to provide an over all view of governance of internet and ethical values of e-governance. It will serve as a dependable reference tool to administrators, policy planners, information technologists, students and researchers.

Editor

Contents

1

Introduction

Governance is not government, nor is it the act of governing. It is more usefully seen as a process: the process by which institutions, organisations, companies and societies 'guide' themselves. It is also about how these bodies interact with each other, with their 'clients' and with the public. At its most basic level, it is about how society organises itself for collective decision making, and also provides transparent mechanisms for seeing those decisions through.

E-governance is a shorthand term for the use and impact of technology, in particular information and communications technology (ICT), in governance systems. How must we adjust the theory and practice of legitimate decision making and policy formulation to meet the demands of a knowledge society?

The change in the landscape of governance in recent years has been dramatic. Technological change has always been with us. What is new is the pace of development. Human knowledge is doubling every seven to ten years. Communication that used to take days now takes seconds. The upheaval this is causing in familiar social, political and economic systems is staggering, still evolving, and by no means fully understood.

For the most part, the institutions and structures of the past are ill-prepared for this new environment. Governments, by their very nature, are especially challenged. Part of the traditional role of government has been to provide a sense of stability in times of change.

Yet the forces for change are too powerful to ignore. Citizens increasingly expect the same level of service from government as they do from other organisations. Businesses transforming their operations for the virtual world are unwilling to go on form-filling and standing in line for government. And the distinctions between agencies of government, business and civil society - and the functions they perform - are becoming blurred as power is distributed and the access costs to connectivity fall.

Thus throughout the world, we see governments, businesses and NGOs working together to bring about e-governance - from Singapore to South Africa, Andhra Pradesh to Washington State, Chile to Estonia. These are not just experiments in new modes of service delivery. As the 'Themes' section makes clear, e-governance inevitably also embraces - and is driven by - new models of policy formulation, new forms of citizenship, new patterns of relationship and power, new options for economic development, and the search for new ways to connect people with the political process.

These developments pose fundamental questions about how governments can act effectively in this new environment in the interests of their citizens and to promote their well-being. It raises questions too about the role and capacity of government, its relationship with its citizens and with other actors. At an even more fundamental level, the connected world raises questions about the boundarics of community, and therefore of representation and citizenship, that go to the heart of democratic theory.

E-governance is beyond the scope of e-government. While e-government is defined as a mere delivery of government services and information to the public using electronic means, e-governance allows direct participation of constituents in government activities. Blake Harris summarizes the e-governance as the following; E-governance is not just about government web site and e-mail. It is not just about service delivery over the Internet. It is not just about digital access to government information or electronic payments. It will change how citizens relate to governments as much as it changes how citizens relate to each other. It will bring forth new concepts of citizenship, both in terms of needs and responsibilities. E-governance will allow citizens to communicate with government, participate in the governments' policy-making and citizens to communicate each other. The e-governance will truly allow citizens to participate in the government decision-making process, reflect their true needs and welfare by utilizing e-government as a tool.

Introduction of e-governance is a key to make information technology (IT) relevant to ordinary citizens in Latin America and Caribbean countries where a large numbers of population are poor and a digital divide is a significant problem. E-governance will allow ordinary people to constantly interface with the government in both local and central level on various matters.

The Bank's involvement in modernization of the government thus is not limited to provide the most advanced Information Communication and Technology to the government so that government can provide its information and service more effectively and efficiently to the citizens. The Bank makes sure that the government will allow all the citizens to access to information or services (any citizens should not be excluded), to articulate their needs and to participate in formulating policy and regulation that will improve their social welfare and well being. The ability of Central government to understand all needs from ordinary local citizens is limited. Therefore, the participation of citizens in local level is extremely important (link with creative community initiative). The true e-governance should be attained by interface of citizens both with central and local government.

e-Government

Similar to the dramatic changes in e-commerce, countries in the Regions have begun to recognize the emergence of e-government —the ability to obtain government services through nontraditional electronic means, enabling access to government information and to completion of government transaction on an anywhere, any time basis and in conformance with equal access requirement—offers potential to reshape the public sector and build relationships between citizens and the government.

At the same time, concerns have already been expressed about the gap between the technology haves and have-nots, and more popularly known as the digital divide. In order to ensure that countries avoid creating a digital divide and create conditions to ensure that growth of the knowledge economy contributes to carrying out a democratic process of efficient, equitable and sustainable development, expanded dialogue and new patterns of cooperation among public, private ad civil society organizations are needed.

The multiple roles of government, at all levels, must be recognized and understood by all if it is to play an effective role in this partnership involving access to information and the role of information and communication technology.

Uses information and information/communication technology provided by the private sector for public administration,

Produces public information to which citizens must have access,

Has the authority to establish marketplace rules and establish regulatory structures that ensure that everyone participates and benefits form growth of the knowledge economy.

There is an inextricable relationship between government's role as a user of information and communication technology and its capacity to formulated public policy for the knowledge economy. Governments that learn how to use these technologies to operate more efficiently and improve public services are more likely to effectively stimulate and contribute to the knowledge economy public policy debate.

Online delivery of services benefits both government and its constituents, as it lowers costs and make services more accessible.

Possible roles for Inter-American Development Bank cooperation in promoting best practices in and e-government.

Latin American and Caribbean countries have already begun to improve public administration through the implementation of e-government capabilities, processes and techniques. The Inter-American Development Bank has been expanding its institutional capacity and knowledge by working with an increasing number of these countries to understand how e-government can be deployed in a manner that is responsive to the special conditions of each country. The Information Technology for Development Division - through our "Digital Democracy" program is facilitating appropriate marches in e-government between the increasing and changing needs of each country and the resources of the Bank.

Creating alliances with other institutions and governments.

Promoting regional dialogue among institutions including different aspects of e-government.

Promoting interamerican cooperation to strengthen democracy through expansion of the e-government capabilities.

e-Government system

In an e-government system we should consider four different possible clients: the government itself (G2G), the employees (G2E), the private sector (G2B), and the citizenship (G2C).

One of the most promising aspects of e-government is its ability to bring citizens closer to their governments. While the technology to facilitate this connection is widely available, many government sites have not taken full advantage of its benefits in Latin American and Caribbean Countries.

Enabling conversation between citizens and government is not the only way to bring citizens and government closer together. Making government more easily accessible is another component of this endeavour. There are few features that make this possible. One of them is the ability to search a particular web site. Another is to offer life broadcast of important speeches through the web. Another way is by enabling citizens to cater available information to their particular interest.

Benefits of e-Government integration

— Lower costs as well as improved efficiency and quality of service.

— More effective linkages between citizens and government.

— Improve efficiency of government workers.

— Facilitate transparency and accountability

2

Understanding E-Governance

Developing country (DC) governments have been using IT for more than 40 years. So what's new about e-governance? What's new is that we are moving on from IT to ICTs and from IT to IS.

New Digital Connections: ICTs: The old model was one of information technology (IT) automating the internal workings of government by processing data. The new model is one of information and communication technologies (ICTs) supporting and transforming the external workings of governance by processing and communicating data. E-Governance should be seen to encompass all ICTs, but the key innovation is computer networks – from intranets to the Internet – creating a wealth of new digital connections:

— Connections within government – permitting 'joined-up thinking'.

— Connections between government and NGOs/ citizens – strengthening accountability.

— Connections between government and business/ citizens – transforming service delivery.

— Connections within and between NGOs – supporting learning and concerted action.

— Connections within and between communities – building social and economic development.

As a result, the focus grows from just parts of e-administration to also encompass e-citizens, e-services and e-society.

New Systemic Approaches: IS: The old models held information technology isolated from the mainstream of reform, or held IT as the objective of reform. The new model brings information systems (IS) to the heart of reform.

In practice this means two things:

— *A central role for ICTs*: as governance becomes – and becomes recognised as – ever more information-intensive, ICTs become an essential part of more and more governance initiatives. ICTs are also recognised as a key lever to change. They are no longer isolated on the sidelines.

— *An integrated role for ICTs:* e-governance means using ICTs as servants to the master of good governance. ICTs are no longer seen as an end in themselves and they are seen to work only as part of a wider systemic 'package'.

Overall, then, e-governance is the ICT-enabled route to achieving good governance. We might prefer to think of it as 'i-governance' – integrated governance – since it integrates both the processing and the communication technologies; and since it integrates people, processes, information, and technology in the service of achieving governance objectives.

E-Governance for Development

As is true all over the world, government in the developing nations costs too much, delivers too little, and is not sufficiently responsive or accountable. Good governance reforms aim to address these shortcomings. Yet progress – after many years of effort in implementing such reforms – has been much more limited than expected. E-Governance offers a new way forward, helping improve government processes, connect citizens, and build interactions with and within civil society. What exactly has e-governance got to offer? At root, it has the power of ICTs, which provide three basic change potentials for good governance for development:

— *Automation:* replacing current human-executed processes which involve accepting, storing, processing, outputting or transmitting information. For example, the automation of existing clerical functions.

— *Informatisation:* supporting current human-executed information processes. For example, supporting current processes of decision making, communication, and decision implementation.

— *Transformation:* creating new ICT-executed information processes or supporting new human-executed information processes. For example, creating new methods of public service delivery.

These change potentials, in turn, can bring – singly or in combination – five main benefits to governance for development:

Efficiency gains

— *Governance that is cheaper:* producing the same outputs at lower total cost.

— *Governance that does more:* producing more outputs at the same total cost.

— *Governance that is quicker:* producing the same outputs at the same total cost in less time.

Effectiveness gains

— *Governance that works better:* producing the same outputs at the same total cost in the same time, but to a higher quality standard.

— *Governance that is innovative:* producing new outputs.

These are the direct and objective benefits. ICTs can bring many others. For example, use of ICTs by government can bring benefits both internally and externally:

— Internally, providing benefits such as better staff motivation or greater political control or an improved public image.

— Externally, by delivering cheaper, better services to those who depend on government. Indirectly by demonstrating the benefits of ICTs to the wider population; by catalysing the local IT industry; and by encouraging foreign investment.

E-Governance does not cover e-commerce and e-business applications that focus solely or mainly on the private sector. As noted above, instead, there are three main domains of e-governance.

— Improving government processes: e-Administration

— Connecting citizens: e-Citizens and e-Services

— Building interactions with and within civil society: e-Society

Respectively, these particularly address the problems that government is too costly, too inefficient and too ineffective; too self-serving and too inconvenient; and too insular.

Such initiatives deal particularly with improving the internal workings of the public sector. They include:

— *Cutting process costs:* improving the input:output ratio by cutting financial costs and/or time costs. Automation can replace higher human costs with lower ICT costs to support efficiency/productivity improvements. Informatisation can support decisions and implementation in downsizing or rightsizing exercises. The rationale is to address the large size of public sector expenditure and/or the inefficiency of many of its processes. The Egyptian case below is an example.

— *Managing process performance:* planning, monitoring and controlling the performance of process resources (human, financial and other). Informatisation supports this by providing information about process performance and performance standards. The rationale is to make more efficient or effective use of process resources. The Tanzanian case below is an example.

— *Making strategic connections in government:* connecting arms, agencies, levels and data stores of government to strengthen capacity to investigate, develop and implement the strategy and policy that guides government processes. Examples of such connections are central-to-local, ministry-to-ministry, executive-to-legislature, and decision maker-to-data store. Automation and informatisation support this by digitising existing information channels. Transformation supports this by creating new digital channels. The rationale is to provide clearer direction for public sector and state processes and to provide for a more evidence-based approach to policy and process. The Chinese case below is an example.

Creating empowerment: transferring power, authority and resources for processes from their existing locus to new locations. Typically that transfer is to lower, more localised levels of the public sector and may be seen as decentralisation. Transformation supports this by creating new information flows to decision makers and process implementers in new locations. The rationale is to reduce the costs and increase the speed of processes and decision making and/or to create more flexible and responsive processes. The South African case below is an example.

Traditionally, ICTs have been used within government in 'automation' mode, replacing clerical labour processes with their digital equivalent. These are essential building blocks for e-governance. However, their achievement of financial cost-cutting goals is questionable. In the North, replacing costly humans with cheap ICTs may cut costs, though even here evidence of productivity gains is limited. In developing countries, replacing cheap humans with costly ICTs is unlikely to be justified on financial cost grounds. As time replaces money as a more critical global resource, ICTs' ability to increase process speed may provide some justification for automation. More generally, ICTs need to be justified and understood in the context of a broader vision and necessity for e-governance. From this base of clerical automation, there are three e-administration trends at work in developing countries:

— ICTs are spreading up the organisation, increasingly supporting the work of operational and tactical managers and, most recently, beginning to touch the working lives of politicians and other senior public officials. As the high water mark of ICTs rises higher, their impact on government increases.

— Use is changing from automation to informatisation and transformation. As the change potential of ICTs increases, they deliver ever-greater benefits and enable ever-greater changes in the process of government.

— From a focus on processing (i.e. computers, the I in ICTs), applications are moving to a focus on communications (i.e. networks, the C in ICTs) and, most recently, to a focus on both processing and communications. As the power and reach of ICTs grows, so does the power and reach of change in government.

A final trend is the move of ICTs from inside to outside government. Although lagging some way behind, it is the 'outside' focus that will be discussed in sections C2 and C3.

Developing Country e-Administration Examples :The examples that follow, and those in subsequent sections, are provided as evidence that e-governance is not only the future in developing countries, it is also the present in developing countries. Why were these initiatives successful? They were successful because they 'kept it simple' and because their design took account of current realities in both their DC host organisation and, where relevant, the external environment.

National ID System in Egypt

In Egypt, the Information and Decision Support Center has created a comprehensive national database with 85 million birth records, 34 million death records, 12 million marriage records and 2 million divorce records. This has provided the basis for a national ID number and, hence, a secure and accurate national ID card. Automation of previously-manual processes has saved considerable sums of money. The information base and ID numbers have also been an essential building block in the creation of other public sector planning and service delivery applications. (IDSC 2000). See also the Tanzania case below.

Delivering Management Control in Tanzania

"The Government of Tanzania has recently launched its integrated HR and Payroll systems covering about 280,000 public servants. While the capital invested was significant at around US$6.5 million, the savings already accrued in improved management – reduced ghost workers, improved control, and accuracy – mean that the project has already paid for itself. The Government of Tanzania has also implemented an Integrated Financial Management System (IFMS) at all ministries in Dar es Salaam and Dodoma via a wide area network. IFMS has improved control over expenditure management, resulting in more timely and detailed reporting. Internet-enabled versions of both systems will soon be rolled out countrywide." (Ntiro 2000).

Sustainable Development Strategy in China

There was a recognition in the Chinese government that formulation and implementation of sustainable development strategies were hampered by lack of adequate information, and that much of the data underlying this information lay scattered in many different organisations. Therefore an ICT-enabled national Agenda 21 network was created, particularly linking a set of key national government, local government and public sector research institutions. The project also helped connect leading decision makers with valuable Web-based data resources on sustainable development. In addition to raising the profile of sustainable development with policy makers, the network has also helped bring faster and more information to the process of strategic environmental decision making. (SDNP 2000a).

Creating Empowerment

Breaking the Apartheid Legacy in South Africa

The ANC-led government in South Africa is making

extensive use of ICTs in its bid to democratise a public sector run for decades largely by, and for, an Afrikaner minority. Attempting to 'reinvent' itself, Johannesburg Metropolitan Council initiated an intranet project. This was intended to break apartheid-legacy information flows and give all staff access to both formal and informal information sources. Careful design (analysed further in section D2 below) ensured that the project was a success. Council processes have become more inclusive and transparent. The project is now being extended to encompass local community leaders as well. (Benjamin 2001)

C2. Connecting Citizens: e-Citizens and e-Services

Such initiatives deal particularly with the relationship between government and citizens: either as voters/ stakeholders from whom the public sector derives its legitimacy, or as customers who consume public services. These initiatives may well incorporate the process improvements identified in section C1. However, they also include a broader remit:

— *Talking to citizens:* providing citizens with details of public sector activities. This mainly relates to certain types of accountability: making public servants more accountable for their decisions and actions. Informatisation and transformation support this by providing the new information flows from government to citizens on which accountability depends. The rationale is to increase the pressure on staff to perform well and to improve public understanding of government. The South Korean case below is an example.

— *Listening to citizens:* increasing the input of citizens into public sector decisions and actions. This could be flagged as either democratisation or participation. The main potential is for informatisation and transformation to support this by providing new information flows from citizens to government. The rationale is to make public decisions more responsive to citizens' view or needs. A South African example is given below, although this relates to the automation of democratic processes, not informatisation/transformation.

— *Improving public services:* improving the services delivered to members of the public along dimensions such as quality, convenience and cost. This uses all the potentials of ICTs to deliver the informational components of public services to citizens in digital form. The direct rationale is clear from the definition, but there is also an indirect rationale of releasing citizen time and money that would otherwise be captured by inefficient service delivery. The Chilean case below is an example.

Because all these initiatives rely on the new connectivity offered by ICTs, they are all relatively new inclusions within e-governance. They are particularly representative of the significant new possibilities offered by e-governance for development. They also represent something of a further chronology of ICT-enabled governance (in addition to those identified in section C1). The chronology starts with *publishing* (delivering data to citizens), then moves to *interaction* (delivering data to citizens and receiving data from citizens), then moves to *transaction* (undertaking other government processes online).

All of these have so far been rather neglected in developing countries, yet even very basic publishing activities can have significant effects. The information poverty of DC citizens is such that they can often be conned into bribery because they lack the most basic information on the who, where and how of government services. Publishing that information on the Web directly attacks information poverty and its effects. Publishing government forms can also have a strong disintermediating effect – cutting out the public servants and others who may illegally charge citizens for access to such forms.

However, the model for disintermediation in the South will not match that in the North. In the North, the main models for government—citizen interaction have been disintermediated models of direct digital connections to the individual citizen. In other words, these are models involving the replacement of human intermediaries by ICT intermediaries. For the majority of citizens in the North, the ICT intermediary is personally-owned (typically an Internet-linked PC in the home or workplace). For many others, the ICT intermediary is institutionally-owned (typically in a local community centre, library, school, post office, telecentre, etc.).

In the South, the first model – citizen direct ownership and use of ICTs – will apply to only a small fraction of the population for the foreseeable future. A greater number will gain access through the second model – non-ownership but direct use of ICTs – through similar institutions to those listed above. Many will also fall into the grey area between these models that is particularly found in the South – direct use of ICTs owned by family, friends, neighbours or colleagues.

Nevertheless, for the medium-term, the majority of citizens will remain on the wrong side of the digital divide. They create a substantial need for a third model – of those who are neither direct owners nor direct users of ICTs. To benefit from e-governance, these citizens will have to rely on reintermediation models that insert a human intermediary between the citizen and the growing digital infrastructure of e-governance. Where institutionally based, these can be thought of as 'intelligent intermediaries' that add human skills and knowledge to the presence of ICTs.

Realistic e-governance for development projects will therefore have to identify and nurture such intermediaries. They may be existing professionals (e.g. accountants for online tax systems; notaries for online registration systems); or public servants (e.g. in call centres or in one-stop-shop government offices); or NGOs and community-based organisations (e.g. staffed community telecentres); or private sector organisations (e.g. cybercafes); or other public institutions. The Gyandoot case in section C3 provides an example – the entrepreneur running the online kiosk frequently goes online on behalf of his/her clients, helping cross the cognitive gap between cyberspace and life in an Indian village.

Greater Openness of Local Government in South Korea

At the highest level in the Municipal Government of Seoul there were concerns about lack of accountability and existence of corruption in the issuing of local government licences and permits. This led to the development of the OPEN system (Online Procedures ENhancement for civil applications): an anti-corruption Web portal that provides citizens with a range of relevant information. This includes the overall goals of the anti-corruption drive and an explanation of the rules and procedures for permit/licence application and processing. However, OPEN goes beyond this. It displays an anti-corruption index that summarises survey results on process performance. It also provides citizens with specific information by allowing them 'real-time monitoring of the progress of an application for a permit or license'.

Some of this information can also be found in paper form but, for the increasing number of Seoul citizens or citizen groups with Internet access, this has reduced the barriers to obtaining government information. They are therefore better informed, the process of government is more open, and the rationale for bribery has been largely removed. Feedback from citizens has been very positive, and there has been a dramatic decrease in reported corruption. In large part, these achievements have been due to the integrated approach taken, ensuring that technological change serves public sector reform goals rather than vice versa. (World Bank 2000a).

Supporting Free and Fair Elections in South Africa

Following difficulties in the 1994 elections, South Africa's Independent Electoral Commission "was charged with making sure that the country's second democratic elections in 1999 were 'free and fair'. This election was vitally important for the stability of the South African political climate and for ensuring that democratic processes were solidly in place. Through large scale implementation of unique information technology applications, the IEC was able to ensure that all South African citizens could have their voices heard. The effort included the creation of a nationwide satellite-based wide-area network and infrastructure; a bar-code system used to register 18.4 million voters in just nine days; a geographic information system used to create voting districts; a national common voters' role; a sophisticated election results centre for managing the process; and the training of 300,000 people. The massive programme was completed in less than two years, in time for the vote." For this, the IEC received the 2000 Computerworld Smithsonian Award for most outstanding programme in the government and non-profit organisations category. (Microsoft 2000)

Better Tax Return Filing for Citizens in Chile

Chile's Internal Revenue Service has taken a typical three-step approach to Web-enabled improvements in services to the public. The first step – publishing – involved static presentation of information on taxation rates, procedures and plans. The second step – interaction – allowed citizens to enter a personal ID number, tax return ID number and password. They could then check on the status of their tax return to see if refunds were due or if the return was still being reviewed. Following the introduction of new legislation, the third step – transaction – allows citizens to file tax returns online and to make subsequent online corrections. There have been tens of thousands of online tax returns and hundreds of thousands of online status checks since the system's introduction. The system has reduced costs and increased speed and accuracy of service. It "saves money on printing, distribution and processing time. And online customers find the system easier, faster, and more accurate than traditional paper-based services. Whereas processing a tax return had previously taken 25 working days ... the new online package was delivering online assessments in just 12 hours." These gains mean 'online taxpayers have an extra 10 days in which to declare their taxes' and they also get refunds 'at least a month before paper-based claimants'. (World Bank 2000b)

Building External Interactions: e-Society

Such initiatives deal particularly with the relationship between public agencies and other institutions – other public agencies, private sector service providers, non-profit and community organisations – and with the relationship between civil society institutions. As with citizen connections, these initiatives may well incorporate the process improvements identified in section C1. However, they also include a broader remit:

— *Working better with business:* improving the interaction between government and business. This includes digitising procurement from and services to business to improve their quality, convenience and cost. This uses all the potentials of ICTs to deliver the informational components of public services to business in digital form. It also includes digital support for opening up government to business through outsourcing and other public—private partnerships. The direct rationale is to drive costs down and quality up within government, but there is also an indirect rationale of improving the efficiency and responsiveness of local business. The Philippine case below is an example.

— *Developing communities:* building the social and economic capacities and capital of local communities. This uses all the potentials of ICTs to strengthen current information connections and to build new information connections within communities and between communities and other institutions. The rationale is to improve the wealth-creation potential and quality of life of community members. The Indian case below is an example.

— *Building partnerships:* strengthening institutional relationships. This has two parts. First, building government partnerships: strengthening relations between government and other institutions such as NGOs or international organisations. Second, building civil society partnerships: strengthening relations between the institutions of civil society, such as between NGOs. This uses all the potentials of ICTs to strengthen current information connections and to build new information connections between institutions. The rationale is to create a strong economic, social and political 'fabric' within society. The Honduran case below is an example.

As with e-citizens and e-services, e-society initiatives rely on the new connectivity offered by ICTs. Thus, they are all relatively new inclusions within e-governance. Again, they are particularly representative of the significant new possibilities offered by e-governance for development.

e-Society – at least relating to communities or to other non-governmental institutions – has been a focus for recent donor-funded 'e-development' initiatives. Why? Partly because such initiatives operate at the institutional rather than individual level, and because they operate somewhat independently of the red tape of government. There has also been a strong e-development interest in government-disintermediating service delivery initiatives. These seek to deliver education and health advisory and other information-intensive services direct without state intervention, often on a North-to-South basis.

Other components of e-society – typically those relating to government links – have been rather more neglected. Thus, as with citizen-focus projects, the opportunity has yet to be fully grasped to use the new connectivity to help refocus the state from an internal, self-serving view to an external, nation-serving view.

Reforming Import Procedures in the Philippines

Both business and government in the Philippines were concerned about the delays and corruption associated with customs and importation. An ICT-based system was introduced to address these concerns. Importers create a single electronic declaration which is processed to calculate payments due and to undertake risk analysis which identifies shipments that may require physical inspection. The online system has allowed a move to cashless procedures in which verification of duty/tax payment is sent electronically from authorised banks to Customs. The verification is automatically reconciled against processed declarations and a release order is then issued. The release order is sent electronically to the Customs warehouses that hold shipments. The result is a much faster service for business. "Cargo is released between four hours to two days, as opposed to eight days in the earlier system." Reconciliation of payments – which used to have a four-month backlog – is now done within the day, and there are fewer errors. Finally, because Customs staff no longer handle cash or physical documentation, the pressures and opportunities for importers to make corrupt payments have been largely removed. (Bhatnagar 2001).

Developing Rural Communities in India

The Gyandoot project set up 31 Internet-connected kiosks in villages in a district of central India where 60% of the population live below the poverty line (earning less than US$1 per day). Each kiosk was initially funded by the local government committee. It is run by a local young entrepreneur along business lines: fees are charged for the services provided. Government-related services include online application for government certificates; online filing of complaints; printing of land records (which are held online and which all farmers need every season to obtain bank loans); and access to information on government welfare and related schemes. Other community development services include: access to agricultural produce prices; an auction site for sale/ purchase of land, equipment and animals; online discussion forums; and e-mail. In the first year of operation, the kiosks were used on tens of thousands of occasions. Proven benefits include better prices for agricultural produce; easier sales of other items; faster reactions to complaints or problems (e.g. an outbreak of cattle disease); and improved knowledge and skills within the communities served. (Bhatnagar & Vyas 2001)

Strengthening Civil Society in Honduras

The Sustainable Development Network is an Internet-linked group of more than 400 institutions that play a leading role in Honduran civil society. It has proven its worth in acute situations. For instance, it was able to act as a clearinghouse for requests for food, medicines, blankets and other supplies in the aftermath of Hurricane Mitch. Sources of supply were identified via the Network, and their delivery was also co-ordinated online. The Network also plays an important longer-term role through topic-based virtual discussion forums, through institution-to-institution information exchange, and through development of online data stores. Given state control of most mass media in Honduras, the Network provides one of the few public spaces for discussion and access to information that is outside state control. This has led to a strengthening of civil society and provided greater opportunities to pressurise government to improve its functioning and transparency. (SDNP 2000b).

Given growth in the new connectivity, e-governance initiatives may increasingly fall into overlaps. An example is given below.

Strengthening Parliamentary Functions in Uganda

The Uganda Parliamentary Technical Assistance Project has placed a heavy emphasis on improving information flows to, from and within Parliament, particularly through use of ICTs. To date, more than half the MPs and many research staff have undergone ICT training; a Web site has been created; and the information capacities of the Parliamentary Library have been expanded. Draft bills can be viewed, budgets and expenditure tracked, and examples of legislation in other countries accessed. Key Parliamentary information can therefore be accessed not just within government but also outside government by citizens, NGOs, and others. "As a result of this modern technology and training, MPs now make requests for research to be carried out and for background information from the Parliamentary Library and Research staff. The effective use of these resources has resulted in new legislative initiatives, better constituent representation, and improved parliamentary oversight of the Executive Branch." The project therefore strengthens connections within government, between government and citizens, and between government and other civil society institutions. (Ugandan Parliament 2000).

The Challenges to E-Governance for Development

The success stories cited above are the exception rather than the rule for two reasons. First, most developing countries have only undertaken a limited number of e-governance initiatives. This mainly relates to a lack of e-readiness, discussed later.

Second, most e-governance initiatives that are begun currently fail. Surveys of e-governance initiatives in DCs are incredibly rare; a shortcoming that needs to be addressed. Even donors, who should be committed to monitoring and evaluation, rarely seem to produce reports. From the material that is available, two main types of e-governance failure can be identified.

In some cases, there is the *total failure* of an initiative never implemented or in which a new system is implemented but immediately abandoned. For example, India's Indira Gandhi Conservation Monitoring Centre was intended to be a national information provider based on a set of core environmental information systems. Despite more than a year of planning, analysis and design work, these ICT-based systems never became operational, and the whole initiative collapsed shortly afterwards (Puri et al 2000).

Alternatively, there is the *partial failure* of an initiative in which major goals are unattained or in which there are significant undesirable outcomes. For example, the Tax Computerisation Project in Thailand's Revenue Department set out seven areas of taxation that were to be computerised. At the end of the project, only two areas had been partly computerised, and five others were not operational (Kitiyadisai 2000).

One type of partial failure that particularly seems to affect e-governance initiatives is the *sustainability failure* of an initiative that succeeds initially but then fails after a year or so. An example is the creation of a set of touch-screen kiosks for remote rural communities in South Africa's North-West Province. These were initially well received. However, the kiosks' lack of updated or local content and lack of interactivity led to disuse, and the kiosks were removed less than one year later (Benjamin 2001). Sustainability question marks also hang over some of the case studies cited above.

As noted, we have only glimpses of evidence about the prevalence of such failure. A few surveys have been conducted, with examples summarised below:

— *Use of ICTs for health reform in South Africa's public sector:* widespread partial failure of high cost systems with little use of data (Braa & Hedberg 2000)..

— Use of ICTs in the Thai public sector: 'failure cases seem to be the norm in Thailand at all governmental levels' (Kitiyadisai 2000).

— Donor-funded public sector ICT projects in China: all were found to be partial failures (Baark & Heeks 1999).

— World Bank-funded public sector ICT projects in Africa: almost all were partial – often sustainability – failures (Moussa & Schware 1992).

Likewise, independent reports on ICT use in the public sectors of individual developing countries find failure to be the dominant theme. It is important to acknowledge that developing countries are not alone in suffering high levels of failure with e-governance initiatives. However, they do face a particular set of constraints that arise from two related challenges: lack of e-readiness and large design—reality gaps.

The Strategic Challenge: e-Readiness for E-Governance

Lack of e-readiness contributes to both lack of and failure of e-governance initiatives. Six key questions can be asked of developing country governments in order to assess how strategically prepared they are for e-governance.

i. Is the Data Systems Infrastructure Ready? Are the management systems, records and work processes in place to provide the quantity and quality of data to support the move to e-governance? In many countries, data quality and data security – for example – are very poor, and there are few mechanisms to address these issues.

ii. Is the Legal Infrastructure Ready? Are the laws and regulations required to permit and to support the move to e-governance in place? In many countries, for example, digital signatures cannot be accepted.

iii. Is the Institutional Infrastructure Ready? E-Governance can only be progressed if the institutions exist to act as a focus for awareness and to act as a means for facilitation of e-governance. In many countries, there are no institutions to co-ordinate and lead and drive e-governance.

iv. Is the Human Infrastructure Ready? Are the attitudes, knowledge and skills in place – especially within the public sector – that are required to initiate, implement and sustain e-governance initiatives? In many countries, key skills gaps relate to business analysis and system design, and to project management, contract management and vendor management. There are also 'mindset' gaps: general resistance to change; lack of customer-orientation; resistance to data-sharing; etc.

v. Is the Technological Infrastructure Ready? Although there have been great strides forward, the fact remains that most developing countries are a long way short of the computing and telecommunications infrastructure on which many Northern e-governance initiatives have been based.

vi. Is the Leadership and Strategic Thinking Ready? A critical pre-condition in successful e-governance for development is an e-champion or small group of e-champions: leaders with vision who put e-governance onto the agenda and make it happen. Cases like those described above show that such leadership can smash through many operational barriers. Conversely, all the operational e-readiness in the world is of limited value if there is no vision and leadership to give direction to e-governance.

Of all the e-readiness issues, then, this is probably the most critical, and it will be addressed in some detail under five headings:

— *No captains on the bridge:* because of lack of awareness, knowledge, skills and confidence there is a generic lack of e-governance leadership and commitment amongst senior public officials. Related to this, there is a dearth of any vision or strategy on e-governance from within many developing countries.

— *One man's meat is another man's poison:* because of the lack of leadership confidence and capacity within many DCs, e-governance initiatives are frequently driven from outside government by vendors or by donors or by consultants. The locus and focus of strategy is therefore not always right. As a result, inappropriate systems are being forced in; systems from other sectors or countries that do not fit specific DC realities. This is a classic case of square pegs and round holes that will be discussed further in section D2.

— *Missing the g-spot:* where donors set the e-governance for development agenda, their strategic focus will be critical. But, as noted above, many recent e-development initiatives from bilateral and multilateral donors appear to be deliberately avoiding government. This is partly because of the human capacity and regulatory constraints within government, and partly because of continuing 'government bad, markets/NGOs good' undercurrents within development. Many such initiatives are therefore bypassing the state and going for community telecentres, ICTs in schools, telemedicine, e-commerce and the like: e-business and non-governmental e-society. e-Administration, e-citizen and e-services initiatives, and the government-related components of e-society – altogether representing the 'Networked Government' model for e-governance – have been too greatly ignored, leaving a growing opportunity gap.

— *Four-Is:* with or without donors, and because of attitude and knowledge gaps, e-governance for development is not being approached properly.

- In some cases, ICTs are ignored – as if they didn't exist; at least some good governance initiatives act as if the last 50 years of ICT development never happened.
- In other cases, ICTs are isolated – separated from the main thrust of the governance project, and so making no effective contribution to it. Ignorance or isolation seems to characterise many identifiable initiatives (see 'current situation' in Figure 3 below). For an example of the latter, one only has to look to the programme structures of major development institutions. Frequently, there will be a structure for governance and a separate structure for ICTs, but no effective communication or synergy between the two.
- In still other cases, ICTs are idolised – put as the centrepiece of governance initiatives, becoming an end rather than a means. This is increasing as

public officials find out about ICTs and/or fall for the vendors' hype (see 'emergent situation' in Figure 3 below). It has something to recommend it – ICTs can be a useful lever to change – but governance goals are often mislaid.

— Only rarely are ICTs properly integrated into good governance reforms, with reform objectives in the driving seat, with information requirements well understood, and with ICTs serving those requirements and objectives (see 'required situation' in Figure 3 below).

— *I'm not listening:* because of attitude and knowledge gaps but also because of cultural and political realities in some developing countries, the strategic approach to key stakeholders (users, clerical operators, citizen beneficiaries, community members) is sometimes ineffective. These stakeholders are sometimes completely ignored in the planning of e-governance projects. Quite aside from any ethical questions, this leads to the direct practical consequence of e-governance failure.

The strategic challenge of e-readiness addresses e-governance at the macro-level of the whole nation as a precursor to e-governance. In addition, though, there is a tactical challenge that faces the micro-level of individual e-governance projects during their implementation. This is the challenge of avoiding failure and achieving success. From a study analysing dozens of e-governance projects, a new model has been developed to explain and predict e-governance success and failure. The model centres around design—reality gaps: the difference between design ideas and organisational realities. The study showed that, the larger this design—reality gap, the greater the risk of e-governance failure. Conversely, the smaller the gap, the greater the chance of success.

For example, taking the case above of an intranet in Johannesburg Metropolitan Council, design and reality were often well matched, along dimensions including:

— *The information dimension:* the intranet was designed to provide just the kind of information that Council users wanted, creating little gap between designed and actual information needs.

— *The technology dimension:* the project plan relied mainly on existing technology within the Council, creating little gap between designed and actual technology.

— *The objectives and values dimension:* the project met the real (sometimes personal) political aspirations of senior councillors and officials, and gained their support, creating little gap between designed and actual objectives.

— *The staffing and skills dimension:* intranet developers had the necessary skills to produce the system that had been designed, creating little gap between designed and actual skill requirements.

— *The other resources dimension:* the project was set up cheaply and incrementally, without particular time pressures, creating little gap between designed and actual resource requirements.

All of this meant only limited gaps between e-governance project design and Council reality. The result was success.

However, as noted, failure has been more common than success, and archetypes of e-governance failure did emerge from the study: situations when a large design—reality gap – and, hence, failure – was more likely to emerge:

— *Hard—soft gaps:* ICTs are often conceived in terms of machinery and engineering, rationality and objectivity. Many e-governance systems get designed according to these conceptions. The trouble is that many government and civil society organisations do not adhere to these 'hard' ideas. In reality, they are dominated by 'soft' factors: people, politics, emotions and culture. When a hard IT design meets a soft reality, there is a large gap, and a strong likelihood of failure.

— *Private—public gaps:* despite the best efforts of 'new public management', the public sector remains fundamentally different from the private sector. This seems to be forgotten by too many ICT vendors, donors and consultants – a particular problem when, as mentioned above, they are often in the e-governance driving seat. They may pick up an information system designed for the private sector. Then they try to shoehorn it into a very different public sector reality. The large design—reality gap generates lots of heat and noise, not much light and, ultimately, plenty of e-governance failure.

— *Country context gaps:* it sometimes seems that only the first half of 'Think Global, Act Local' gets remembered. Designers seeking quick fixes try to pull e-governance solutions off-the-shelf from other countries. But New York is not New Delhi, and

Kuala Lumpur is not Kingston. So there is often a large design—reality gap when trying to introduce in country X an e-governance system designed for country Y. The frequent result is failure.

Strategy and Tactics for E-Governance

E-Governance lies at the heart of two global shifts: the information revolution and the governance revolution. Both shifts are changing the way society works and the way that society is governed. They bring the opportunity for not just incremental but radical gains in efficiency and effectiveness.

But, at present, any such benefits are accruing to the few, not the many. It is the few who have access to ICTs, to digital information and knowledge, and to the benefits of reform in governance. We can thus talk of an 'E-Governance Divide' that is increasingly separating developed and developing countries, and elites and ordinary citizens within developing countries. This growing divide must be addressed if the poor in developing countries are not to fall even further behind. We must seize the digital opportunity for governance and seize it now. Delay for the South as the North pushes ahead will only reinforce historical patterns of inequality.

So ... what must be done? In short, there must be both a strategic and a tactical response that attacks the current challenges to e-governance for development hard and head-on.

At the tactical level of individual e-governance projects, identified best practice on design—reality gap closure must be adopted. Examples of such best practice include (Heeks forthcoming):

— *Legitimising and mapping current reality:* integral to e-governance project success is an understanding of reality. Yet this may be difficult to achieve. E-Governance project leaders can help by 'legitimising reality': by encouraging stakeholders to articulate the difference between rational, prescriptive models of what they should be doing and real depictions of what they are actually doing. Techniques for exposing and mapping organisational realities play a role here. Self- and third party observation helps expose realities. Use of soft systems tools such as 'rich pictures' helps map realities. Prototyping helps both, particularly helping users to understand their real information needs.

— *Customisation to match realities:* as described above, e-governance solutions designed for one sector or country are being forced directly into a very different reality, creating failure. To combat this, leaders of e-governance projects must be competent enough and confident enough to demand designs that match their situation's unique reality. The keywords for such projects must be 'customised' not 'off-the-shelf'; 'adapt' not just 'adopt'.

— *Modularity and incrementalism:* with the growth in connectivity and as a natural consequence of dealing with millions of entities, e-governance projects are frequently large. With pressures from donors/ vendors and pressures to play catch-up with the private sector, e-governance projects are frequently ambitious. But, the bigger and bolder the project, the greater the risk of failure. Designers must reconfigure such projects to limit the extent of change at any given time. Stretching project time horizons is one technique. There is also a growing consensus behind modularity (supporting one business function at a time) and incrementalism (providing stepped levels of support for business functions) within e-governance projects.

— *Hybrids and terminology:* design—reality gaps often arise because of a 'two tribes' mentality. IT designers understand technology but not the realities of governance. Officials and politicians understand the realities of governance but not the technology. 'Hybrid managers', who understand both perspectives, are the answer. Yet hybrid training is practically non-existent. Worse, the tribal gap is growing with increasing outsourcing of e-governance work to the private sector. This exacerbates the clash of culture and values between designers and users. Terminology, too, is part of the problem. 'E-Governance' (electronic governance) may be unhelpful by suggesting, wrongly, that delivery of ICTs is an end in itself. As stated above, it may be more appropriate to talk of 'i-Governance' (integrated governance or, perhaps, intelligent governance) that places governance objectives in the driving seat, with ICTs seen as one part of the means to deliver those objectives alongside people, processes and information.

Closing specific gaps: as well as applying generic best practices such as those just described, it will also be important to address specific design—reality gaps. Early analysis of these gaps in e-governance projects

> means moving beyond the narrow confines of typical risk assessment models, with their focus on the simple parameters of project resources. It means, instead, converting each of the ITPOSMO dimensions into a set of rating scales. Key project stakeholders then discuss and score these scales. The whole process can be undertaken as a facilitated workshop with an iterative approach. The major design—reality gaps are identified, and the workshop then moves to work out how to close those gaps. This process can become even more iterative if it forms part of a cycle of learning and reflection during the project.

In summary, the cases analysed in this chapter show that e-governance has a key role to play in current and future development. It can offer critical improvements to the efficiency and effectiveness of governance; and probably offers critical future legitimacy for government. The issue for developing countries, therefore, is not 'if e-governance' but 'how e-governance'.

In addressing the 'how', this chapter has shown that improvements and legitimacy will only be delivered if two things are in place. First, the strategic e-readiness infrastructure, especially the leadership and integrated vision on which e-governance depends. Second, the tactical best practices that are needed to close design—reality gaps and to steer e-governance projects from failure to success.

Democratic and Accountable Governance Structures using ICT

The penetration of Information and Communication Technologies (ICT) in all facets of human existence is leading to changes in the way humans interact within the society and the way societies involve individuals in the evolution process. Societies are increasingly getting transformed to Knowledge Societies and its inhabitants into Knowledge Networkers who are more informed of the events happening locally and globally. Their actions are based on the strong foundation of knowledge which is universal, objective, timely and triangulated from various sources. The people are becoming more aware of their rights and opportunities that lie ahead of them and are developing capabilities to make an informed Choice in all areas which influence them, including the sphere of Governance.

In this wired-up era, the inhabitants of the Knowledge Societies will have all the more freedom, flexibility and opportunities to decide how they would like to be governed and by whom. The underlying truth will become self-evident that- it is not the leaders who govern people but it is the people who let the leaders govern them.

Information and Governance

It is a well-acknowledged fact that access to information plays a critical role in setting up of Governance/ Control mechanisms. This process is founded on extraction and accumulation of information and using it to the effect which creates hierarchal structures on which power gets unequally distributed. The skew in the distribution of the power is proportional to the critical information residing at each hierarchal level.

Some facts pertinent to Information and Governance are:

— Access to Information and Knowledge forms the basis of decision-making and concerted action.

— Judicious and well-informed decision-making is dependent on the quality and timeliness of information.

— Circumscription of information and knowledge with a few levels opens up avenues for its manipulation for exploitative purposes.

ICT and Governance

ICT can influence the process of Governance in various ways and and in varying degrees, from improving the current mechanisms of delivery of services to transforming the entire mechanism and the nature of services themselves. The role played could be:

— purely Technical in terms of automation of tedious tasks earlier done by humans,

— to a Facilitating / Supportive role leading to more participatory and all encompassing decision-making and implementation processes,

— to a completely Innovative role which involves new services and new mechanisms to deliver these services.

Digital Governance

Digital Governance is a popular term to focus on the new, evolving forms of governance - Electronic Governance. Good Governance rests on the pillars of knowledge and recognition of this set of knowledge by the decision-makers. Digitisation of this entire set of knowledge within a network which links every individual including the decision-makers and gives democratic freedom to everyone to access and make use of this knowledge paves the way for Digital Governance.

Introduction of Digital Governance is a way to ensure that common citizens have equal right to be a part of decision-making processes which affect them directly or indirectly, and influence them in a manner which best improves their conditions and the quality of lives. The new form of Governance will ensure that citizens are no longer passive consumers of services offered to them and would transform them to play a decisive role in deciding the kind of services they want and the structure which could best provide the same.

Models of Digital Governance

Models of digital Governance are still evolving and improvising themselves to fully harness the potential offered by the new Information and Communication technologies. Based on my secondary research, I was able to identify a few generic models which are shaping up. These models are based on the inherent characteristics of the new technologies which are: enabling equal access to information to anyone who is a part of the digital network and de-concentration of information across the entire digital network.

In simpler terms, information does not reside at any one particular node in the Digital Governance Models but flows equally across all the nodes- a fundamental change from the current information hierarchal information flows which led to unequal distribution of information and hence skewed power-relations.

— Generic Models (click for more details)

— Broadcasting / Wider-Dissemination Model

— Critical Flow Model

— Comparative Analysis Model

— E-Advocacy/ Lobbying and Pressure Group Model

— Interactive- Service Model

These models exhibit several variations dependent on the local situation and the nature of governance activities conducted through these models.

Broadcasting / Wider-Dissemination Model

The model is based on dissemination of governmental information already available in the public domain into the wider public domain through the use of ICT and convergent media.

The strength of the model rests upon the simple fact that a more informed citizenry is better able to understand the functioning of the governance mechanism and is therefore more empowered to exercise its Rights and Responsibilities. It opens up an alternate channel for people to access information as well as validate information available from other sources. The widespread application of this model corrects the situation of Information Failure and provides people with the basic governmental information to make an informed decision.

This model could be applied in the following possible ways:

— Putting Governmental Laws and Legislations online.

— Making available the names, contact addresses, emails, fax numbers of local/ national/ regional/ international government officials online.

— Make available information pertaining to Governmental Plans, Budgets, Expenditures, and Performances online.

— Put key Judicial decisions which are of value to general citizens and create a precedence for future actions online. viz. key Environmental Decisions, State vs. Citizen decisions etc.

Critical - Flow Model

The model is based on the principle of disseminating/ channeling information of critical value (which by its very nature would not be disclosed by those about whom it is about) to a targeted audience (such as the media, opposition parties) or into the wider public domain through the use of ICT and convergent media.

This model requires a foresight to understand the "strategic use value" of a particular information set and locating users to whom the availability of the particular information set would make a critical difference.

The strength of this model is the fact that ICT makes the concept of distance and time redundant, and this could be used to the advantage by transferring the critical information to its strategic user group located anywhere or by making a critical information set available in the wider public domain.

This model could be applied in the following possible ways:

— Making available Corruption related data about a particular Ministry / Division/ Officials online to its electoral constituency or to the concerned governing body.

— Making available Research studies, Enquiry reports, Impact studies commission by the Government online to the affected parties.

— Making available Human Rights Violations of the Government or allied authorities online for access by Judiciary, NGOs and concerned citizens.

— Making available Critical Environmental Information available to local inhabitants such as radioactivity spills, effluents discharge, information on green ratings of the company etc.

Comparative Analysis Model

Comparative Knowledge Model is one of the least-used but a highly influential model that is gradually gaining acceptance. The model, if used innovatively, can fully harness the potential and capacity offered by the rapidly expanding Information and Communication Technologies and aim it towards better governance.

The model is based on exploring information available in the public or private domain and comparing it with the known information sets to derive strategic learnings and arguments. Essentially, the model continuously assimilates new Knowledge Products and uses them as a precedence or benchmark to evaluate, influence or advocate changes in current policies and actions. The comparison could be made over a time scale to get a snapshot of the past and present situation or could be used to compare the effectiveness of an intervention by comparing two different situations.

The strength of this model lies in the infinite capacity of ICT to store information in a retrievable manner and transmit it almost instantaneously across all geographical and hierarchal barriers; and the potential of ICT enabled Knowledge Networking Processes.

Applications/ Possible Projects

This model could be applied in the following possible ways:

— To learn from historic policies and actions and derive learning lessons for future policy-making.

— To evaluate the effectiveness of the current policies and identify key learnings in terms of strengths, flaws and policies.

— To effectively establish conditions of Precedence, especially in the case of Judicial or legal decision-making (example for resolving patent-related disputes, public goods ownership rights), and use it to influence/ advocate future decision-making.

— To enable informed decision-making at all levels by enhancing the background knowledge and providing a rationale for future course of action.

— To evaluate the performance and track-record of a particular decision-maker/decision-body.

E-Advocacy / Mobilisation and Lobbying Model

E-Advocacy / Mobilisation and Lobbying Model is one

of the most frequently used Digital Governance model and has often come to the aid of the global civil society to impact on global decision-making processes. The model is based on planned, directed, strategic flow of information to build strong virtual allies to complement action in Real World. It takes up a pro-active approach of forming virtual communities which share similar values and concerns, promoting active sharing of information within and between these communities, and linking them with real-life groups/ activities for concerted action. The model creates synergies between real-world processes, and opinions and concerns expressed by virtual communities.

The strength of this model is in its diversity of the virtual community, and the ideas, expertise and resources accumulated through this virtual form of networking. The model is able to mobilise the potential of human resources and information overcoming geographical, institutional and bureaucratic barriers, and target them for concerted action.. Further, it provides a strong virtual arm to many of the activities done by organisations/ communities in real world. The model is often used to direct e-campaigns against a particular individual or decision-making body.

This model could be applied in the following possible ways:

— Fostering public debates on issue of larger concerns, namely on the themes of upcoming conferences, treaties etc.

— Formation of pressure groups on key issues to force decision-makers to take their concerns into cognisance.

— Making available opinions of a suppressed groups who are not involved in the decision-making process into wider public domain.

Catalysing wider participation in decision-making processes.

Building up global expertise on a particular theme in absence of localised information to aid decision-making.

Interactive-Service Model (G2C2G)

Interactive-Service model is a consolidation of the earlier model and opens up avenues for direct participation of individuals in the governance processes. Fundamentally, ICT have the potential to bring in every individual in a digital network and enable two-way / interactive flow of information amongst them. The potential of ICT for the governance is fully leveraged in this model and leads to greater participation, efficiency and transparency in functioning of the government as well as savings in time and costs relating to decision-making.

The model makes possible the various services offered by the Government to be made directly available to its citizens in an interactive manner. In a way, it opens up an interactive Government to Consumer to Government (G2C2G) channel in various functions such as election of government officials (e-ballots); grievance-redressal; sharing of concerns and providing expertise; opinion polls on public issues etc.

This model could be applied in the following possible ways:

— To establish an interactive communication channels with key Policy- makers and members of Planning Commissions.

— To conduct electronic ballots for the election of government officials and other office bearers.

— To conduct public debates / opinion polls on issues of wider concern before formulation of policies and legislative frameworks.

Filing of grievances, feedback and reports by citizens with the concerned governmental body. Performing governance functions online such as revenue collection, filing of taxes, governmental procurement, payment transfer etc.

3

Governance of the Internet

It is now well recognized that the global network environment, and in particular, the Internet, defies traditional regulatory theories and governance practices. The main reasons are linked to the disintegration of the concepts of territory and sectors.

It has therefore been suggested to approach the regulation of the Internet from different points of view, technical, self-regulating and legal, for instance.

This chapter is a first exploration of those challenging issues, but does not pretend to be more than an attempt to assess what is really happening in the different domains of technical mechanisms, self-regulation and the law.

We are not looking at what could be done, but at what is done through those different instruments. trying to enlighten which are the ethical issues which are covered by those instruments and which are not. It is a kind of a first inventory.

Ethical issues and questions with filtering software

Filtering/control software is a technical means, located on a PC or a server or at the level of an Internet service provider, to restrict the distribution of certain kinds of material over the Internet. In many cases, its goal is the protection of children against sex, violence, hate speech, etc.

Table 1: Labeling categories and their frequency in a sample of 10 ratings

Labeling categories	Frequency in the sample
sex	7/10
violence	7/10
age	5/10
intolerance/hate speech	5/10
gambling4/10	
drugs	3/10
language	3/10
nudity	3/10
alcohol/tobacco	2/10
profanity2/10	
education content	2/10
gross depictions	1/10
satanic/cult	1/10
militant/extremist	1/10
quality 1/10	
etc.	

This kind of software is promoted or supported by industry, Free Speech activists and some governments. Currently a lot of the available control software packages filter at the level of the entry point to an address on the basis only of their proprietary (and secret) list of URLs.

But this could evolve thanks to PICS (Platform for Internet Content Selection). PICS is a set of technical standards which have been developed since summer 1995 by the MIT's World Wide Web Consortium. "The first and most important distinction that PICS introduced is a separation between labeling and filtering.

A label describes the content of something. A filter makes the content inaccessible to some audience." In other words, thanks to PICS, "Consumers choose their selection software and their label sources (called rating service) independently." "More generally, there are six roles that could be filled by different entities", as explained in table 2.

Table 2: The 6 roles implied by filtering software (according to Resnick 1998)

1. Set labeling vocabulary and criteria for assigning labels
2. Assign labels (= rate or classify)
3. Distribute labels
4. Write filtering software
5. Set filtering criteria (= customize)
6. Install/run filtering software

Moreover, PICS standards facilitate "self rating (enable content providers to voluntarily label the content they create and distribute) and third party rating (enable multiple, independent labeling services to associate additional labels with content created and distributed by others. Services may devise their own labeling systems, and the same content may receive different labels from different services."

PICS would become more and more important. Control software such as Cyber Patrol does not hesitate to become currently PICS compliant. PICS approach, which separates clearly the different roles involved in filtering, helps to analyze issues and allows solutions which are interesting from an ethical point of view.

Ethical issues with filtering software will be discussed here from the breakdown of table 2. Let us first remark that to set labeling vocabulary and criteria for assigning labels is not value-neutral and that to assign labels and to set filtering criteria imply moral judgments. Any ethical approach has thus to focus on these three roles.

Outside PICS

Outside PICS, it happens as a rule that several roles (particularly to set criteria for assigning labels or for classifying, to assign labels, to distribute labels and to write filtering software) are filled in the framework of one firm or even by one sole commercial entity.

Ethical issues are obvious with this kind of software: users are linked to the subjective value judgments of this firm ! Even to set filtering criteria can be reduced by the firm to a nearly virtual role: the only choice available can be, for example, between filtered access or not filtered access.

Within PICS

Within PICS, as explained above, the six roles can be filled by different entities. This can obviously improve the situation from an ethical point of view but cannot delete any issue.

We suggest here a set of questions to be raised and which, of course, remain valid outside PICS.

Set labeling vocabulary and criteria for assigning labels

To set labeling vocabulary and criteria for assigning labels is a crucial role. First it influences automatically other steps of the filtering process (assigning labels and setting filtering criteria). But moreover, as pointed out by CPSR (1997), "in general, the use of a filtering product involves an implicit acceptance of the criteria used to generate the ratings involved."

- Who is in charge of this role ? Is the identity of the person or the body responsible for this role clearly given in the documentation about the filtering software ? Would it be justified that a government fills this role ?
- Are the rating vocabulary and criteria clearly defined so as to allow the user (parents, ...) to judge if they are consistent with his/her own values ? Are they rich enough to allow a real choice at the level of the rating and at the level of the customization ?

Assign label

- Who is in charge of the very sensitive role of assigning labels ? Is the identity of the person or the body responsible for this role clearly given in the documentation about the filtering software ?

- Which of the two approaches (self-rating and third party rating) is the best ?
- When a third party rating service is involved, the next questions are to be raised: Who is effectively represented by this third party ? Is this party representative, for example, of a values-oriented organization or of a given population or culture? How are the ratings attributed?
- With self rating, the questions are: How to oblige or, at least, to incite people to self rate? And on the basis of which principle? How to solve the problem of mislabeled pages, and particularly of deliberately mislabeled pages? As suggested by Cranor & Resnick, "The Internet community will need to co-operate in the creation of either vouching services, which vouch for authors who are honest in their self-labeling, or blacklisting services which keep track of authors whose labels are not reliable."
- If people assign labels and if labeling is not compulsory all over the world, it is obvious that many sites will stay unlabeled. The question is then: What to do with unlabeled sites? If the software allow unrated sites, then the global control will not be efficient but if it does not, then innocuous and very interesting sites will be not accessible (see the discussion of Weinberg on this subject). And thus in this case, "blocking software could end up blocking access to a significant amount of the individual, idiosyncratic speech that makes the Internet a unique medium of mass communication. Filtering software, touted as a speech protective technology, may instead contribute to the flattening of speech on the Internet."

- Can the person or body in charge of the rating use rating criteria in accordance with his/her own value judgments ?
- Are the ratings numerous and various enough to cope with the diversity of cultures and of opinions at the level of the customization ?

Set filtering criter

- Which kind of customization? In fact there is a dilemma: the more choices you give to the final users the more difficult it is to set! A solution in the future could be, as suggested by Cranor & Resnick, "to allow users to download preconfigured setting from organizations they trust. Child advocacy organizations as well as various religious, political, and educational organizations might recommend configurations to parents. Parents could download these settings with a simple click of the mouse and have them installed into their childs software."
- Who is in charge of this role? Initially this role was dedicated to parents to control their children. But filtering software are used also by libraries (in the USA), for instance to control adults, by schools and by firms. Is it ethically justified to give such a power of control to this kind of entity? "A government could try to impose filtering criteria in several ways, including government-operated proxy servers (a national intranet), mandatory filtering by service providers or public institutions, ..." Would it be ethically justified ?
- Can the person or body in charge of the customization find both criteria and a rating in accordance with his/her own value judgments?

Governance and Self-regulation

Pierre Van Ommeslaghe defines self-regulation as "a legal technique according to which the legal rules or the rules of conduct are created by the persons to whom they are intended to be applied, - either those persons do it by themselves or they are represented to do it", but he does explicitly exclude some 'codes of conduct' which are enacted by international organizations, since the persons to which the code will be applied are not participating in the process. In a way which is not very different, Pierre Trudel defined it as "the recourse to voluntary norms which are developed and accepted by those who participate in a determined (specific) activity."

Our Corpus - Different styles

We have gathered some 15 documents - codes or rules - which may be relatively well recognized as self-regulatory instruments of governance for the Internet to which we joined the 30 IFIP Codes that we had analyzed before. Our collection shows the extreme diversity of the material which comes under the label 'self-regulation'. We tried to classify the documents according to the Van Ommeslaghe's classification but we were obliged to consider it as inapplicable. The present list is more classified on themes or names.

The 'Ten Commandments' and the Netiquette rules

- The Ten Commandments of Computer Ethics, by the Computer Ethics Institute (CEI), Washington, D.C.; published in many places.

- Suggestion of Netiquette - Core Rules of Netiquette, Virginia Shea.
- The Net: User Guidelines and Netiquette, by Arlene H. Rinaldi.
- Charter and Guidelines for news.admin.net-abuse.announce, Source: Newsgroups: news.admin.net-abuse.announce, 11 April 1995.
- One planet, One Net: Principles for the Internet Era, CPSR (Computer Professionals for Social Responsibility): still under discussion. (not analyzed)

Charters

- Cyberspace and the American Dream: A Magna Carta for the Knowledge Age, 1994, published by the Progress and Freedom Foundation (PFF).
- Online Magna Charta, Charta of Freedom for Information and Communication, 'The Wartburg Charta', 1997.
- The Intergovernmental Information Technology Leadership Consortium (Council for Excellence in Government) - Draft - Consortium Charter, 1997.

Codes of Ethics and Conduct

- Codes (Standards/Guidelines) of Ethics (Practice/Conduct) of IFIP Computer Societies.

ISPs', SPA's Codes, 'Virtual communities' rules and others

Codes of ISPs' (Internet Service Providers) Associations

- Internet Service Providers Association (ISPA-UK), Code of Practice, 1996.
- Internet Service Providers Association (ISPA-Belgium), Code of Conduct, 1998.
- Canadian Association of Internet Providers (CAIP), 1997.
- La Charte française de l'Internet, Proposition de Charte de l'Internet, Règles et usages des acteurs de l'Internet en France, 1997.
- La Charte de l'Internet proposée par la France à l'OCDE, Proposition française présentée à l'OCDE pour une Charte de coopération internationale sur Internet, 23 octobre 1996. (not analyzed)

'Virtual Communities'

- JANET Acceptable Use Policy, 1995.
- GeoCities Members Guidelines, and particularly GeoCities Page Content Guidelines and Member Terms of Service, 1998.

Others

- US SPA's (Software Publishers Association) Guidelines for Copyright Protection (previously called 'ISP Code of Conduct'), 1997.
- International Chamber of Commerce, Guidelines for ethical advertising on the Internet, 1998.

Most of them are short, maximum 2 A4 pages; but some are shorter than others; 10 commandments, 10 rules of Netiquette, 7 principles for the Internet era. Symbolic figures! And sometimes one stresses that it must be a 'portable' regulation: CPSR doesn't hesitate to launch its idea 'One planet, one net' on a book marker! It seems that that the shortness is a characteristic of such kind of documents, except when they are 'codes of practice'. But this shortness has, at least, to be combined with the content density!

A tentative analysis

The 'Ten Commandments' and the Netiquette rules

The first series of texts is a mix of prevention against what is called computer crime (for the Ten Commandments) and of kindness and fairness (for the Netiquette rules). Many of the rules governing Newsgroups, for instance the 'Charter for news.admin.net-abuse.announce', are worth being mentioned since they make explicit what is considered as "net-abuse", and which is spelled out, at least partially, in terms similar to those used in computer crime laws.

The categories of computer crime which were adopted by the Council of Europe in 1990 may fix our attention and cover the majority of the topics here suggested. The Council of Europe recommended to have a Minimum List, which includes computer related fraud, computer related forgery, damage to computer data or programmes, computer sabotage, unauthorized access, unauthorized interception, unauthorized reproduction of a protected computer programme, unauthorized reproduction of a topography, and an Optional List covering alteration of computer data or programmes, computer espionage, unauthorized use of a computer, and unauthorized use of a protected computer programme.

The Charters

'Cyberspace and the American Dream: A Magna Carta for the Knowledge Age' is a manifesto of the Progress and Freedom Foundation (PFF), in the spirit of the third wave of the Tofflers. If we mention this 'Carta', it is only to notice the hot issues as they are seen by certain zealous propagandists: property rights necessary for the market, infrastructure ownership, dynamic competition on the Cyberspace marketplace and Schumpeter's 'creative destruction' with its winners and losers, customized and actionable knowledge for the Knowledge Age, hackers "vital for economic growth and trade leadership", ...

The 'Online Magna Charta, Charta of Freedom for Information and Communication, The Wartburg Charta' (1997), is no more than the previous one, a 'Charter'. It is a protesting reaction of Netizens when the US CompuServe provider blocked the access to 200 discussion fora under judiciary inquiry, in November 1995. It is a claim to the right to free speech and the freedom of opinion, information and communication, the right to 'a virtual home'.

The last 'charter' here mentioned is the 'Intergovernmental Information Technology Leadership Consortium Charter' which again does not fit into that category and is more a self-satisfactory statement promoting its own quality in the delivery of government services, in the economic growth, and in the citizen participation at all levels of the process of governance.

Codes of Ethics and Conduct

Codes of Ethics and/or Conduct of many computer

societies, such as in IFIP, are not specific to the Internet, but their content is rather frequent in such a kind of self-regulation and so worth noticing.

The 'fields of reference' which have been considered by at least one third of the 30 codes of the IFIP national member societies which we have examined are as follows :

- Respect for the interests or rights of the people involved, for the prestige of the profession, for the interests or rights of the public, for the welfare, health of the public, and for the quality of life;
- Conscientiousness and honesty, acceptance of responsibility and integrity, respect for requirements or contracts or agreements, conscientious work, professional development and training , competence, effectiveness and work quality;
- Confidentiality, privacy in general and respect for property rights;
- Flow of information to involved parties, and information to the public;
- Respect for the code, for the law, and for IT and professional standards.

ISPs', SPA's Codes, 'Virtual communities' rules and others

Our collection of self-regulatory documents still include 4 Codes of Internet service providers associations, 2 'virtual communities' rules, 1 Software publishers association Guidelines for Copyright protection, and 1 International Chamber of Commerce Guidelines for ethical advertising on the Internet.

Codes of ISPs' Associations

The 'French Proposal of an Internet Charter' must be included in the category of ISPs' codes, more than in the charters' category. On the opposite, the 'US SPA's Guidelines for Copyright protection', although it was called earlier 'ISP Code of conduct', will be mentioned in our last category 'Others'. The French proposal - still a draft - is the most complete one, and also the longest: it is more than 12 pages long whilst the others are generally 2 pages. It seems also that in Europe, at least among the 10 EuroISPA members, there are only 2 having presently a code. So, our collection contains, first, 4 codes of ISPs' Association: two Europeans (UK and Belgium), one Canadian, and the French draft.

The comparison regarding the people concerned and the country does not reveal great mysteries: the members of the association and the country where it is located! Let us just mention the CAIP's Code which stipulates that "it will cooperate with international organizations and law enforcement authorities ..." Procedures for enforcement are not very strong, and the commitment for reporting is weak.

As the topics are concerned, at the risk to be regarded as nationalist, let us take the most recent code, from Belgium. Except the French draft, it is the most complete and it includes most of the items of the others. It includes general commercial clauses insisting on legality and sincerity (services, products or advertising material), honesty (with clients; inform them of this existing code), personal data protection, publicity, and right information on prices. These commercial clauses are spelled out in similar terms in the UK and Canadian documents. There are also special clauses on crime in the

Belgian code: pay special attention for fighting against 'illegal or dubious material', but no capacity for controlling everything; they will assist public authorities, have special email address for complaints, and inform hotline about every illegal or harmful transaction: sex, pornography, paedophilia, racism, xenophobia, genocide denial, provocation or encouragement to criminal act, criminal association, gambling and lottery, drugs ("list is not closed"), ...

What the draft French Internet Charter seems to bring new in the scope is the creation of what is called an 'Internet Council', "an independent and unique body for self-regulation and mediation." Its roles will include information and advice to actors and users, process of complaints, and participation in the international cooperation. The role is a bit larger than the ISPs associations. The Canadian association of Internet providers code resembles to the others, but one specific clause is worth mentioning: "CAIP members are committed to public education about Internet issues and technology (f.i. how to assign liability for content and network abuse, and help all Canadians understand the options available to all stakeholders).

'Virtual Communities'

JANET is the well known UK education and research community network. We do not have here a real document of 'self-regulation', but an 'acceptable use policy', as it is most of the time called in Anglo-Saxon world. But it contains rules which are typical not only of such academic community, but of many others: privacy protection, no harmful material, no computer crime (unauthorized access, no defaming, no infringement of copyright, corrupting or destroying other users' data, disrupting the work of others, other misuse of JANET or networked resources, such as the introduction of 'viruses', etc.), and also some rules of usual Netiquette such as: "Do not use JANET for deliberate activities such as wasting staff effort or networked resources, (...) in a way that denies service to others, ...

JANET acceptable use policy is a very temperate and sober community code when compared to the GeoCities Guidelines. GeoCities could be classified among the ISP, but it looks also like a big community - 'more than 2 million GeoCitizens' from all the world, located in some 40 'Neighborhoods' - common interest communities.

Regarding the illegal or harmful material, the rules do not differ very much from what we have read until now. "Refrain from using free Personal Home Page or GeoCities Chat and Forum session for: material containing nudity or pornographic material; material grossly offensive to the online community, including blatant expressions of bigotry, prejudice, racism, hatred, or profanity; material that exploits children under 18 years of age; restricted or password-only access pages, or hidden pages or images (...)."

There are other interesting clauses. "Refrain from: instructional information about illegal activities, physical harm or injury against any group or individual, or any act of cruelty to animals; defaming any person or group; for commercial purposes (...); using page (or directory) as storage for remote loading or as a door or signpost to another home page."

The list includes a clause which is nearly the copy of one from the US SPA Guidelines for Copyright Protection, as we shall see: "refrain from using your home page for acts of copyright, trademark, patent, trade secret or other intellectual property infringement, including but not limited to offering pirated computer programs or links to such programs, information used to circumvent manufacturer-installed copy-protect devices, including serial or registration numbers for software programs, or any type of cracker utilities (this also includes files which are solely intended for game emulation)."

Then it goes on with: "Refrain from: violating Internet standards for the purpose of promoting your home page; hyperlinking to content not allowed in GeoCities; gathering personally identifiable information for commercial or unlawful purposes; posting or disclosing any personally identifiable information belonging to children. [Kids: For your safety, do not put your real name, address, phone number, e-mail or other information like that on your webpage or give it to strangers.]"

This rather long list is completed by an explicit sentence: "GeoCities does not actively monitor the content of Personal Home Pages but will investigate complaints of violation of these guidelines.

Others

We have finally collected two specific Guidelines, because they are 'sectoral' and linked to the Internet.

The first one, the Guidelines of the US SPA are in a way curious, because they have been developed by SPA for server operators who do not seem "to participate in the activity", to quote the definition of self-regulation by Pierre Trudel: the real actors on whom self-regulation is here imposed are the subscribers. The question was very controversial: SPA suited small ISPs, but the case was dropped. Amusingly, when writing this paper, we found a 'Hotnews' 'Dutch ISPs Refuse to Squeal on Software Pirates': "Dutch Internet service providers World Access/ Planet Internet, XS4All and Euronet have said they will not check their systems for advertisements by software pirates, even though the Business Software Alliance (BSA), an organization of software distributors, holds the providers responsible for the majority of software piracy over the Internet in the Netherlands." The subject is surely hot and on the agenda of many organizations, as well as the general problem of intellectual property right.

The Guidelines of ICC on Advertising and Marketing on the Internet are surely worth seeing, since we are here also in a very sensitive domain. The privacy protectors and the anti-spamming leagues will surely react to such guidelines. Problems which are here treated are: legality, honesty, social responsibility, clear information to the users, use of personal data (with a right to opt-out), right to access his/her own data, no unsolicited commercial message (when indicated), special clauses for advertising to children, and respect for potential audiences: pornography, violence, racism, sexism, ...

Self-regulation : first results

What could be considered in some way as a tedious analysis reveals repetitions and a rather convergent final result. Some 'issues', if not 'categories', emerge:

- fairness and kindness: Netiquette, ISPs, ICC

- respect, honesty, competence, sincerity, right information, ...: Codes, ISPs, ICC
- privacy (and deriving rights such as right to know about his/her own data): nearly all
- computer crime: Ten Commandments, Net-abuse administration, Virtual communities, Janet, ICC
- intellectual property right, copyright, trademark, patent, ...: GeoCities, PFF Carta, US SPA
- free speech, right to information and communication: Wartburg, French Charta
- illegal, dubious, harmful material: ISPs, GeoCities, ICC
- etc.

We must say our disappointment about the other features of our analysis: people involved and concerned, places where self-regulation is applicable, rules for enforcement. It looks like the reign of vagueness.

About enforcement and procedures, without doubt, we are in a relatively recent situation: the texts we have examined do not go back further than 1994-1995. Moreover, as most often, organizations do not like to report on complaints which could reveal a weakness in their security system, for instance. This means that we shall have difficulties to evaluate the functioning of the procedures, when they exist. We can just regret that some organizations explicitly state that they cannot commit themselves in controlling what they have on their servers.

This means that, if the topics and issues appear relatively clearly, the main concern, in terms of governance, reveals that we have to make further decisive progress. We could also add that the real problem with such codes is not that they exist, but that in some pages they try to cover what the law needs many well crafted numerous articles for!

The Internet : the role of the law. Two new legal issues

The problem of the regulation of the Internet could be solved in different ways. The law is one of them. But, because of the particular nature of this new medium, and especially the fact that it allows to exercise a lot of different fundamental freedoms (like the freedom of expression, the freedom of information, etc.) important ethical choices have to be made in order to conciliate all interests.

To give a better idea of these ethical choices, we will analyze the regulation chosen in two different topics: the protection of privacy and the protection of copyrights.

The protection of privacy

Different choices have been made in USA and in the European Union. These choices could be explained in an economical point of view. On the one hand, we have the United States of America whose economical tendency is liberalism, which means that the market should be let free to solve as much issues as possible. On the other, the European Union which has chosen to regulate.

The choice made in the United States

In July 1997 the Clinton's Administration published a

paper entitled : Framework for global electronic commerce" in which different principles were developed from which three are relevant for our purpose.

First of all the private sector should lead and consequently, the government will encourage industry self-regulation and the private sector participation in the making of standards or collective agreements. Secondly, Governments should avoid undue restrictions on electronic commerce. Thirdly, where governmental involvement is needed, its aim should be to support predictable, minimalist, consistent and simple legal environment for commerce which means that the Governments plans to set up only decentralized or contractual model of law rather than a legal environment base on top-down regulation.

The choice of the federal administration was clearly in favour of self-regulation. But in 1998, a poll taken by Business Week revealed that a lot of citizens refused to go online because of privacy concerns. The efforts of the companies to set up adequate privacy protection seemed not to be convincing. It is why in July 1998, the Federal Trade Commission made the following declaration : "Unless industry can demonstrate that it has developed and implemented broad-based and effective self-regulatory programs by the end of the year, additional governmental authority would be appropriate and necessary."

One month later, the Federal Trade Commission charged the company GeoCities, one of the most popular sites on the World Wide Web, of misrepresenting the purposes for which it was collecting personal identifying information from children and adults. A few days later, the GeoCities shares lost more than 20 percents. And that can be considered as a mirror of the growing awareness that Internet privacy protection can have an enormous impact on a company's bottom line.

The choice made in Europe

The legal policy in the European Union has clearly been a regulatory policy. A general directive was issued in 1995 and set up different rights such as the right of access or the right to object.

The general directive speaks also about the self-regulation, and one article is really interesting to understand the place the self-regulation should take (mostly the Codes of Conduct). The article provides that: The Member States and the Commission shall encourage the drawing up of codes of conduct intended to contribute to the proper implementation of the national provisions adopted by the Member States pursuant to this Directive, taking account of the specific features of the various sectors. The Commission seemed to consider the Code of Conduct only as a supplement to the law, nothing more.

This article also creates the possibility for trade associations and other bodies representing other categories of controllers to submit the code they have drawn up to the opinion of the national authority. The Directive suggests that the Member States should make provision for this authority to ascertain whether the drafts submitted to it are in accordance with the national provisions adopted pursuant to the Directive.·

But at this point of the debate we have only compared the choice made in the United States and in the European Union. It would be interesting to join them face to face. The first feature of this confrontation is the article 25 of the European Directive, which provides that : the member States shall provide that the transfer to a third country of personal data which are undergoing processing or are intended for processing after transfer may take place only if, without prejudice to compliance with the national provisions adopted pursuant to the other provisions of the directive, the third country in question ensures an adequate level of protection the second paragraph of the article gives more details about the assessment of the level of protection saying that particular considerations shall be given to the nature of the data, the purpose and duration of the proposed processing operation or operations, the country of origin and country final destination, the rules of law, both general and sectoral, in force in the third country in question and the professional rules and security measures which are complied with in that country. At that moment the level of protection in the USA has been considered as inadequate. But the problem is that the Directive will have direct effect in October 1998. Therefore, US and EU officials are meeting to discuss ways of avoiding a potential impediment to electronic commerce trading between the two continents.

The problem is now: How to solve this conflict? Because both parties will stay on their positions. A solution could may be found in the article 26.2 of the European Directive which creates an exception where the controllers adduce adequate safeguards with respect for the protection of privacy specifying that such safeguards may in particular result from appropriate contractual clauses. So the solution could be the creation of standard contracts which would be used for each transborder data flows to third countries.

In 1997, the Commission issued a second Directive on privacy, particularly focused on the telecommunications. This Directive gives several rights to the consumer with regards to the use of telecommunications, which can be made with a commercial purpose. For example, article 10 says that a subscriber must be provided, free of charges, with the possibility to stop automatic call forwarding by a third party to his or her terminal. These calling systems include the fax transmission, so doing; the Directive provides a solution to the problem of commercial harassment.

In conclusion, we can observe that the process used in the European Union is exactly the contrary to the one adopted in the USA. In a first step, the Clinton's Administration had given the priority to the self-regulation. But recently they have faced different abuses of the market due to the lack of regulation. They probably will come to the decision to write a law. But something remains surprising. It is the fact that the financial market has started to consider the protection of Privacy as a criterion to evaluate a company carrying business in electronic commerce. Therefore it could be considered that a change of the way to regulate privacy in the USA would be the result of an economical choice more than of an ethical one.

European Convention for the Protection of Human Rights and Fundamental Freedoms. The choice of the Commission was to end

On the opposite, the European union started directly with a directive whose purpose was, among others, to ensure a high level of protection to the right recognized in article 8 of the force that ethical value with a Directive but with a possibility to use self-regulation as a complement. It could be asked which of those two process is the most efficient. The answer could be none of them because they both try to stay between the over-regulation and the legal emptiness knowing that each of them is really close to the farthest utmost point.

The protection of copyrights, the competition between law and technology

Opposite to the privacy domain, the field of copyright has been regulated strongly in the USA and in the European Union. The ethical choice has been done in favour of a real protection of the rightholders. But, new questions arise now with the coming out of technical systems of protection. These systems are capable of managing the access to the works.

Furthermore, a proposal for Directive on copyright and related rights in the information society would require Member States to provide adequate legal protection against any activities, including the manufacture or distribution of devices or the performance of services, which would enable or facilitate the circumvention without authority of effective technological measures designed to protect copyrights and related rights."

This position of the Commission is the starting point of different considerations. First of all, the danger is that such an Electronic Copyright Management System (ECMS) could manage the access to works, which are not protected anymore by copyrights. Which might, according to different authors, result in appropriation of public domain, which has to remain freely accessible to the general public."

Furthermore, the technology seems to offer a better protection than the copyrights themselves, and one could ask if that technology will not cause the death of the copyrights in the virtual world? This remark could be found excessive but something is certain, the spirit of the protection by the copyright is changing. Before the protection was an a posteriori one the copyright was invoked after the infringement. Now, to prevent the ECMS to violate the right of information of the public, it becomes necessary to decide a priori which works are protected and which are not.

It is interesting to note that the emergence of the new information technologies could be regulated by three different instruments : first of all the law which has the advantage to be effective and possibly enforced by a court order. But, the law has also weaknesses such as its general character which does not help when practical details have to be solved. The second way to regulate is the self-regulation. This way is generally chosen in sectors where the connections between the actors are very strong like for example in the financial world. The self-regulation has an effectiveness when it is the commercial advantage of the actors to comply with. If it is not, it is really difficult to imagine that such a regulation could have any possibility to be enforced.

A third and new way to regulate is the technology which can integrate the requirements of the law and enforce them by technological ways. The danger resides in the following question: Who is entitled to write the standards governing the machine? Because if only an oligarchy decides of the rules to be implemented by the machine they give to the law their own interpretation and sometimes bypass completely the philosophy of the rule. If, like some authors said the answer to the machine is the machine, the user has to remain the master and may not become the slave Ö

There is a general agreement on the ethical issues as they are covered either by the technical means, or by self-regulation, and partially at least by the law. Privacy (and deriving rights such as right to know about his/her own data); computer crime; intellectual property right, copyright, trademark, patent; free speech, right to information and communication; fight against hatred speech, racism, and against sectarianism; pornographic, illegal, dubious or harmful material; etc. All these issues are rather frequently mentioned.

Within the ways those issues are solved, or at least approached, there are also ethical choices to be clarified. Who is setting the labeling vocabulary and the criteria for assigning labels, who is rating the web sites ? Who is establishing the filtering criteria ? Those questions that we have raised about the technical means show us that there are social and ethical choices. As we have seen there are also ethical and social choices in the ways privacy may, for instance, be protected. Or it may be that a technical choice deregulates the legal means - what is also an ethical and social choice!

Ethics is not out of scope in the governance of the Internet, and plays its role. Therefore, as it was suggested during the recent IFIP-TC9 international conference on Human Choice and computers, we must "care about the net" instead of fearing it, play a role in a more face-to-face way (E. Lévinas); in other words we must devote ourselves to "netmaking" more than to "networking" and we have to create an ethical community. Others were suggesting to strive to develop cross-cultural values to the service of great causes such as reducing violence and promoting peace. Or, to develop principles of governance which include social responsibility. Social dialogue, cultural dialogue, social responsibility are not only important words: they must be in the forefront of our action to create human networks in the age of globalization.

4

Building E-Governance Awareness

E-Governance is the use of information and communication technologies to support good governance. It moves beyond old 'IT in government' models thanks to the new digital connections that ICTs permit. These new connections strengthen existing relationships and build new partnerships within civil society. E-Governance therefore embraces:

— *e-Administration:* improving government processes by cutting costs, by managing performance, by making strategic connections within government, and by creating empowerment.

— *e-Citizens and e-Services:* connecting citizens to government by talking to citizens and supporting accountability, by listening to citizens and supporting democracy, and by improving public services.

— *e-Society:* building interactions beyond the boundaries of government by working better with business, by developing communities, by building government partnerships, and by building civil society.

The emphasis of current private sector and donor initiatives has been on e-business and on non-governmental e-society. This has left a large and growing opportunity gap around the other areas of e-governance. These areas are being largely ignored, to the detriment of development. It is these areas that form the NeGI priorities. The areas noted – e-administration, e-citizen and e-services initiatives, and the government-related components of e-society – together represent a Networked Government model for e-governance.

The vision guiding such initiatives is that developing countries can and must accelerate the pace of e-governance and build networked governments. By doing this, they will reap the benefits of government that costs less, delivers more, and is more responsive and accountable.

If action is not taken, the poor in DCs will be left on the wrong side of an ever-widening divide: not just a digital divide of access to new technology, but a divide of information, of knowledge, and of governance. Countries in the North and elites in the South will be the winners, and the poor in the South will be the losers as inequalities grow.

The overall aim of an NeGI is to more effectively utilise ICTs for good governance reforms. For e-governance to succeed in developing countries, 'e-readiness' must be built. This means the barriers to e-governance must be reduced by strengthening infrastructural inadequacies, and the drivers must also be strengthened. The priority for an NeGI is therefore to build e-readiness in six areas:

— Institutions

— Laws

— Leadership and commitment

— Human capacities

— Technology

— Data systems

The specific objectives of an NeGI are therefore:

— To develop the high-level awareness and commitment that will carry forward e-governance for development.

— To develop the capacities necessary to address e-governance strategically.

— To develop the human and data infrastructure necessary for e-governance pilot projects.

— To implement a number of 'networked government' pilot projects.

By addressing barriers and drivers, an NeGI provides a structured approach and a package of measures that will deliver the following outcomes for those countries that adopt it:

— Awareness and commitment to e-governance at a high level.

— A set of key e-governance institutions that can strategically plan and facilitate e-governance projects.

— New laws and regulations that enable e-governance.

— A national E-Governance Strategy.

— The operational capacities to implement e-governance pilot projects.

— A set of e-governance pilot projects focused on 'networked government'.

One aim of this chapter is to identify ways in which donor agencies can support e-governance for development at a regional or global level. Potential cross-national activities are therefore described for most stage components. Together with national actions, these could be regarded as a complete e-governance 'start-up' package: a five-year programme for e-governance. If so, assuming involvement of six developing country partners in each of which two or three e-governance pilot projects would be launched, then total donor costs would be between US$15m and US$25m depending on the activities undertaken by the donor.

However, it must be recognised that e-governance is a long-term project more likely to be measured in decades rather than years in order to reach down into the heart of governance in developing countries. Any five-year package represents just a small start.

There is no 'one best way'; each country, each organisation must be helped to find its own 'best way'. Lessons can be learned by developing countries from the experience of Northern nations. Lessons can be learned by one DC from the experience of other DCs. But complete blueprints cannot be transplanted.

Rather, a process must be put in place; a process of dialogue, learning, capacity building and facilitation. For the sake of clarity, this chapter provides a description of stages and components. However, this should be seen – at most – as an initial skeleton framework for discussion, not as a cut-and-dried blueprint. Some of the content may not be appropriate in some contexts, and it should not be used prescriptively. A significant part of the localisation of any e-governance initiative will be working out its relationship with existing initiatives and institutions. In particular, some countries may find it beneficial to ring-fence e-governance and give it a clear, separate identity. Others may find it artificial to put a boundary around e-governance and may prefer to take a more holistic approach to the role of ICTs across the whole nation.

Without external encouragement, e-governance initiatives may never be contemplated or started. Without internal ownership, e-governance initiatives may never be developed. Without external facilitation, e-governance initiatives may never be successfully implemented. E-Governance proposals must grapple with the difficult business of balancing and integrating these three forces. Alongside a due concern with partnership, ownership and dialogue, there must be an attempt to identify and trigger change drivers, some of which may lie outside government and even outside the individual nation.

Developing countries already have e-governance and ICTs

This should not be treated as virgin territory; as something the North knows about and South does not. ICTs have been in use by DC governments for the past 40 years. There are regional centres of expertise. There are vibrant, rapidly-growing national IT sectors. Developing nations are awash with e-development projects and proposals. All of this must be recognised and respected. It must also be remembered that the largest e-governance failures have happened in the North.

ICTs must be integrated with, and driven by broader governance objectives. Whilst recognising that ICTs can be valuable lever to reform, NeGI components must take governance objectives as the starting point, using ICTs as a means to those ends not as an end in themselves. ICTs will be one key tool in helping meet the need for reengineered information systems the governance reform demands.

In recognition of the need to integrate ICTs with people, processes and information, and the need to integrate all of these within the broader direction given by governance goals, it would therefore be more appropriate to talk of 'i-governance' – integrated governance – rather than the technology-biased 'e-governance'.

E-Governance projects must show sensitivity to the reality of DC values, structures, infrastructure, etc. Pulling Northern and/or private sector solutions off-the-shelf and trying to impose them will drive square pegs into round holes. E-Governance solutions must be adapted not simply adopted, to ensure that the design of those solutions matches Southern realities. More detail about design—reality gaps, and best practice on closing such gaps can be found elsewhere.

Participative approaches to projects can be a Northern imposition that mismatches Southern cultural and political realities. Nevertheless, as a prophylactic against failure, key e-governance project stakeholders (users, clerical operators, citizen beneficiaries, etc.) need to be more involved – at least talked to and listened to – than they currently are.

Notwithstanding the notion that priorities should not be pre-judged, the NeGI concept does take 'networked government' to be the core current priority within e-governance for development. Why? For two reasons: a) government still lies at the heart of the development process; b) the recent round of donor e-development initiatives has largely ignored these areas, yet the new connectivity means they provide a major opportunity for DC governments.

Evolutionary steps are likely to succeed; revolutionary leaps are likely to fail for both technological and human reasons. E-Governance projects should build carefully and sustainably on the existing ICT usage base. Projects like cyberballots via WAP should go to the bottom of the in-tray; projects like delivering government information to NGOs via e-mail should go to the top. Chronologies such as those described in the related paper are of relevance here: from automation to informatisation to transformation; and from publishing to interaction to transaction. As well as setting the likely trajectory for e-governance, these are also a reminder of the starting point for those who understand we must walk before we can run.

The National E-Governance Initiative

The Initiative as outlined below envisages some form of national Unit to co-ordinate e-governance. Prior to the creation of such a Unit, however, there needs to be a seed institution to administer and co-ordinate the initial processes, like those outlined in Stage 1. This could be seen as a national, regional or international body – with more or less input from donor agencies – that would help 'get the ball rolling' in individual countries. It might cover tasks like running any E-Governance Summit, and initial awareness-raising.

There will certainly be a value in co-ordination at the supra-national level to help in the sharing of experiences and expertise. Opportunities for such cross-national activity – quite possibly donor-supported – are identified and emphasised within this chapter. Such cross-national inputs could be seen as informal/one-off or they could be seen as the rationale for a regional or global 'E-Governance Co-ordinating Centre' that would be created from the outset.

Stage 1: Building E-Governance Awareness and Commitment

Target Deliverables: top-level political and resource commitment to e-governance from each participating organisation; overview guidance document of shared vision and priorities for the National E-Governance Initiative. This would be the official launch event for a National E-Governance Initiative. The Summit could have three main objectives:

— to raise awareness of and build commitment for e-governance in the country,

— to secure national and international resources for e-governance initiatives, and

— to create a document laying out process and structure, programme and project priorities for the National E-Governance Initiative, including any targets.

Such man event would need to be based on considerable data-gathering on local e-readiness (as noted above, the institutional, legal, human, technological and data infrastructure) plus local needs, priorities and views.

Significant pre-Summit activity would be required to build the constituency, the agenda, the ownership and the commitment to the Summit process. Depending on stakeholder politics, this might involve considerable negotiation around frameworks such as the one presented in this chapter and/or their locally-contextualised equivalent. It would also involve positioning and dovetailing vis-à-vis other existing and planned national ICT strategies and initiatives.

In addition to the Summit, other mechanisms would need to be used to raise awareness and commitment among senior officials. These would include the President, Prime Minister, Ministers, Permanent Secretaries and leaders of other institutions of civil society who largely determine whether and how change takes place. By addressing both government and civil society leaders, drivers to e-governance are created both inside and outside government.

To raise awareness and belief that e-governance is relevant, functioning e-governance projects can be identified. The e-governance pilot projects (see Stage 4) would become incorporated into this activity as they came on-stream.

Specific project activities could be to:

— undertake an identification exercise of appropriate existing Demonstrator Sites,

— fund development and maintenance of objective Web-based materials that allow for 'virtual visits' to the Demonstrator Sites, and

— fund physical visits to Demonstrator Sites linked to relevant regional/national training events and other meetings.

A danger of demonstrators must be avoided – the tendency to identify only vanguard/state-of-the-art technology applications and/or the tendency of sites to drift towards 'bleeding edge' applications under pressure from politicians, users and vendors. The problem here is that such applications cannot be applied in the majority of contexts. The emphasis must, instead, be on practicable, usable, replicable applications, and the emphasis must be more on the human and organisational aspects than on the technology. Terminology such as 'i-Governance-in-Practice Site' or 'i-Governance Replicator' may be more appropriate than 'E-Governance Demonstrator'.

One-to-one coaching

Although trivial in many ways, lack of hands-on confidence with ICTs can be a significant problem for leaders that undermines their commitment to e-governance. For senior officials, private and personalised training will be required. In order to sustain skills and confidence, direct and continuing use of ICTs will be beneficial. For example, there could be an arrangement to provide e-mail links (to family or senior national and international leaders) or for intranet access to key documents.

Awareness-Raising Among the Donor Community

Target Deliverable: e-governance components within programmes of major in-country donors.

A package of activities could be delivered that includes:

— seminars and training workshops for donor agency staff,

— Web-based documentation,

— individual meetings with key donor personnel, and

— support for monitoring and evaluation of donor e-governance projects.

The overriding objective would be to create donor partners for the National E-Governance Initiative. Other key objectives within donor agencies would be:

In general within development agency staff there is too little awareness of, and confidence with, ICTs. This needs to be addressed in the usual ways – by training, by seminars, by guidance and advice.

It may also need to be addressed structurally: for example, ensuring that ICTs are not seen as the priority/ preserve of just a single group or department but as something that touches the work of all groups and departments.

Ensuring that some of the best practice principles are adopted, particularly the notion of an integrated approach to ensure that ICTs are not ignored or isolated in development projects, but are integrated as a key tool for meeting project information needs.

As well as training, seminars, guidance and advice, this may also need to be addressed structurally: for example, ensuring that there is some structural mechanism for bringing together 'hybrid' expertise that covers information/ICTs and specific development priorities, such as governance or public sector reform.

Knowledge Building on E-Governance

There is a need for knowledge-building by better (or even just some/any) monitoring and evaluation of e-governance projects. This will be hard work. Firstly, M&E is consistently ignored for both rational and self-interested reasons of donors. Second, this is a particular problem in relation to ICTs. Because they have not followed some of the basic principles identified above, the majority of donor-supported e-governance projects have failed either wholly or partially. Not surprisingly, donors do not want this broadcast and have therefore been very reticent to conduct proper independent evaluation of ICT-related projects. This reticence means that projects are consigned to the 'Groundhog Day' of constantly repeating the mistakes of the past.

Stage 2: Building E-Governance Strategic Capacity

Target Deliverable: existence of strategic and capacity-building E-Governance institutions.

A single focal point for e-governance strategy – something like a 'National E-Governance Unit' – will be needed, responsible for areas such as:

— setting overall e-governance priorities;

— leading the development and implementation of framework policies, standards and guidelines;

— promoting cross-cutting e-governance infrastructure and applications;

— acting as a focus for learning about e-governance;

— possibly providing consultancy/facilitative inputs to individual e-governance projects

Institutions covering these responsibilities may already exist but others may need to be created. Each Unit would ideally also have an e-governance advisory board including not only government members but also representatives of key civil society institutions. Through this or other means, it would also need to be integrated with broader/other national ICT initiatives.

Donor/cross-national inputs could include:

— Advisory inputs on the structure and responsibilities of National E-Governance Units.

— Regional or global E-Governance workshops to provide the basis for knowledge exchange and partnership building between Units.

— A central Web site with e-mail list support to provide a central locus for continuous interaction between Units, and to act as a pool for e-governance experiences.

— Funding for Unit membership of key international e-governance forums (such as ICA: the International Council for IT in Government Administration) since this provides a key opportunity for knowledge- and partnership-building.

National Academies of Excellence in E-Governance

A single focal point for knowledge- and skill-building for e-governance – something like a 'National Academy of Excellence in E-Governance' – will be valuable. Its key responsibility would be to provide training of relevance to e-governance: the emphasis – at least over time – might need to be less on generic ICT skills and more on the broader range of competencies required for e-governance.

Specific training initiatives are described elsewhere, with target groups that would include current political/ civil society top-level leaders, second-tier public officials, current e-governance leaders, future e-governance leaders. Given the importance of leadership a separate *Directorate for E-Governance Leadership* could be included within the Academy. Other Academy activities could include:

— Collaborating with other national, regional and international institutions to collate and disseminate best practices in e-governance: policies, strategies, replicator projects, case studies, and stories.

— Collaborating with the National E-Governance Unit to provide consultancy/facilitative inputs on individual e-governance projects.

Institutions equivalent to these Academies, or equivalent to their holding institutions, may already exist but others may need to be created. Donor/cross-national inputs could include:

— Advisory inputs on the structure and responsibilities of National Academies of Excellence in E-Governance.

— Regional or global E-Governance workshops to provide the basis for knowledge exchange and partnership building between Academies.

— A central Web site with e-mail list support to provide a central locus for continuous interaction between Academies.

— Trainer training for Academy staff.

— Funding for Academy technological infrastructure.

National E-Governance Champions Forum

These would be national bodies drawing together those responsible for e-governance initiatives within individual major public ministries and agencies. The Forum could be responsible for:

— sharing knowledge about best practices in e-governance,

— providing mutual support and sustaining commitment,

— facilitating cross-cutting e-governance initiatives,

— advocacy of e-governance within the public sector and civil society, and

— advising the National E-Governance Unit and/or Academy.

Donor/cross-national inputs could include:

— Advisory inputs on the structure and responsibilities of National E-Governance Champions Forums.

— Regional or global E-Governance workshops to provide the basis for knowledge exchange and partnership building between national Forums.

This Forum could be a loose (potentially virtual) association of those involved with e-governance from the public sector, private sector and NGO sector. Its existence is based on the need to provide solutions that are sensitised to specific national and public sector realities. Forum responsibilities would be:

— to shape national e-governance priorities;

— to disseminate to the national representatives of the private sector and donor community details of best practices for developing and implementing e-governance systems;

— to learn and adapt generic lessons of ICT use in the private sector and donor community and to disseminate those to the public sector. Donor/cross-national inputs could include:

— Encouragement for donor participation in Forum meetings.

— Funding for initial meetings of the Tripartite Forum.

As already noted, the need to create new institutions may be less than indicated: not all may be appropriate to the particular national context; and the functions of some or all may already exist within existing institutions.

Legislative Infrastructure for E-Governance

Target Deliverable: necessary legislative and regulatory changes to facilitate e-governance. E-Governance requires a range of legislative changes including electronic signatures; electronic archiving; data matching; freedom of information; data protection; computer crime; and intellectual property rights legislation. Regulatory changes are required for a host of activities from procurement to service delivery.

All changes would typically form part of broader change to support generic e-economy and e-nation initiatives. In order to support this process, donor/cross-national input could be to host a Web-based resource providing details of legislation and regulatory changes passed in various countries. It would also provide independent commentary analysing the content and impacts of those changes. This would support the work of National E-Governance Units who would drive forward the process of legislative change.

Leadership and Commitment for E-Governance

Target Deliverable: a critical mass of strategic knowledge and skills within government, sufficient to support an e-governance strategy. In addition to awareness-/ commitment-raising activities for top-level leaders, there is also a need to train others who will take a leading role. Training activities to be provided by the Academies could include:

- — E-Governance training for second-tier government and civil society leaders, focusing on building awareness, confidence and commitment to the e-governance process, allowing them to provide high-level inputs and support for e-governance.
- — Leadership training for current e-governance leaders, focusing on their abilities such as leadership, interpersonal skills, strategic planning, and awareness of best practice. The US 'Excellence in Electronic Government Initiative' provides a model for this. Donor/cross-national inputs could include:
- — Co-ordinated development of appropriate ICT-based distance learning materials.
- — Funding of pilot training events for use as curriculum development mechanisms.

Given the centrality of government to e-governance, current (and future) leaders are likely to be principally drawn from within government. Other institutions, though, should not be excluded:

— *Unions*: though often politicised, these may play an important role in either blocking or facilitating e-governance initiatives. Bringing union leaders onside will help progress with e-governance.

— *Civil society*: leaders from the other institutions of civil society can also be usefully included in activities to build leadership and commitment for e-governance.

Future e-governance leaders

Given the lack of e-governance leaders in developing countries, there is a pressing need to develop the next generation of leaders, who can champion e-governance from their current and future positions. This work could be undertaken by the National Academies. Donor/cross-national inputs could include:

— Encouragement for the incorporation of e-governance components into existing 'Young DC Leaders'/'Next Generation' initiatives.

— Organisation of national or regional e-governance seminars and networking events for 'rising stars'.

— Facilitating development of digital support communities for next generation e-governance leaders.

Building E-Governance Strategy

Any national drive for e-governance must be directed if it is not to become fragmented. Therefore, the NeGI should support the development of a National E-Governance Strategy. This could combine the priorities set by any E-Governance Summit with knowledge of particular national priorities and capacities, including other national ICT initiatives and policies. Donor/cross-national inputs could include:

— Maintenance of a Web-based resource on existing ICT/Governance/E-Governance policies and strategies, with a commentary on best practices and impacts.

— Organisation with local partners of national Strategy-Making Workshops that would aim to set out the main contents of strategies.

— Provision of advisory inputs to the Workshops.

Stage 3: Building E-Governance Implementation Capacity

There is a huge e-readiness gap between the capacities needed for pervasive e-governance and the capacities actually present in most developing countries. Completely closing that gap would be a mammoth undertaking. Therefore a suggested priority is to focus on those institutions involved in any E-Governance Pilot Projects. Target Deliverable: adequate human capacity for e-governance in the organisations likely to be affected by E-Governance Pilot Projects.

Training

In general terms, priority human capacities for e-governance are 'hybrids': those who understand the technology *and* the business of governance *and* the role of information in governance. It is they – as individuals or small teams – who can most successfully champion e-governance in the target organisations. Key implementation capacities to be developed for pilot projects would be likely to include:

— Capacity to develop information systems.

— Capacity to manage projects and to manage change.

— Capacity to be an 'intelligent customer': able to raise project finance, specify needs, manage procurement, and manage vendors.

— Capacity to operate and maintain information systems.

Training should also give a high priority to attitude change since a key stumbling block to e-governance is the lack of motivation amongst those involved. Such training should aim to speak to both 'hearts and minds'. Academies of Excellence in E Governance or their equivalent, would be likely to play a lead role in the training to develop human capacities. Donor/cross-national inputs could include:

— Capacity-building interventions with the Academies

— Co-ordinated development of appropriate ICT-based distance learning materials.

— Funding of pilot training events for use as curriculum development mechanisms.

— Support for monitoring and evaluation of training in order to foster best practice.

Conventional training approaches, which have tended to dominate training institutions in developing countries, have relatively limited value. The NeGI could therefore usefully support more innovative approaches. Donor/ cross-national inputs could include:

— Funding and advisory inputs for pilot 'learning projects' adopting more learner-centred acquisition of skills and knowledge: learning diaries, learning sets, work shadowing, job exchanges, and secondments.

— Funding and advisory inputs for pilot 'training projects'. Donor-funded consultancy has been heavily criticised for too often creating inappropriate solutions whilst simultaneously failing to develop local human capacities. An alternative approach is the training project. Training projects turn conventional consultancy on its head, taking the external role from core to periphery and from consulting to training and facilitation. Local staff, ideally from within the target organisation, undertake the work for the e-governance project. External staff do not undertake the work directly, but are responsible for training and facilitating local staff as necessary. Given the advances in ICTs, some of this external role can be undertaken off-site. This ensures that local capacities are built and that local staff – who may have a better understanding of local realities – take the lead.

E-Governance relies heavily on competent public sector staff. But training initiatives and acquisition of on-the-job competence are continuously undermined by the flow of specialist staff out of the public sector. Indeed, ICT-related training can increase the outflow. This could severely compromise the progress of e-governance in the pilot project organisations, and it needs to be addressed by the NeGI. Donor/cross-national inputs could include:

— Funding and advisory inputs for pilot projects adopting innovative HR approaches to the problem. These could include recruitment bonuses, use of Web-based recruitment, and part-public/part-private working weeks. It could also include creation of an E-Governance 'Hit Squad' – potentially all or part of the National E-Governance Unit – that would be regarded as an autonomous unit and paid at market rates.

— Funding and advisory inputs for pilot projects adopting innovative public—private partnership approaches that reduce reliance on the public sector. These could include outsourcing, partial-privatisations/joint ownership, private finance initiatives, and the like.

Infrastructure for E-Governance Implementation

Target Deliverable: a sound ICT infrastructure in the organisations likely to be affected by E-Governance Pilot Projects. Development of ICT infrastructure is an area already being addressed by numerous donor, government, NGO and private sector initiatives in developing countries. The technology has been over-emphasised to the detriment of other components of e-readiness, and it will therefore not be separately discussed here in any great detail.

Institutionally, it could well be valuable to explicitly separate out responsibility for the technical infrastructure underlying e-governance to a national ICT Infrastructure body which would have infrastructural responsibilities across all areas of ICT application, not just e-governance. Bodies with this type of function already exist in several developing countries. The intention is to ensure that the E-Governance Unit is not distracted from its work on strategy, structures and processes, and that it retains the understanding that technology is the servant of good governance. The ICT Infrastructure body, as well as planning and overseeing the roll-out of technology, would also need to focus on the standards and policies (for example on public key infrastructure, on interoperability, etc.) needed to make the technology usable.

Greater reliance on intermediaries (both ICT-owning institutions and humans) must be recognised as a reality in developing countries given that ICT ownership is not an option for most people. Technological initiatives need to recognise this and incorporate identification and support for intermediaries within the public, private and NGO sectors.

Data Systems for E-Governance Implementation

Target Deliverable: more robust data systems in the organisations likely to be affected by E-Governance Pilot Projects. E-Governance projects will rely to a significant degree on existing data, existing systems and existing processes. Where these are already in a mess, addition of ICTs just creates a faster, more expensive mess. Alongside – or even preceding – introduction of ICTs for the E-Governance Pilot Projects, there may therefore need to be moves to reconstruct and renew the underlying data systems.

Existing and planned good governance reforms ought to address this problem. In some ways, they can, through their work to reconstruct work systems and work processes. Unfortunately, they frequently pay too little attention to data issues, and they regularly fall foul of garbage in, garbage out data quality problems. This may well point to the need for support for existing data-centred initiatives, and also data sensitisation of existing governance projects. This means, for example, strengthening the information systems component of existing public sector reforms, and ensuring that information systems are not just equated with ICTs, so that an integrated approach is followed. Part of that integrated approach should be a recognition of the 'humanity of data' – the fact that data quality, data security and data sharing depend, at root, on human motivations and values. Donor/cross-national inputs could include:

— Encouraging donors to pay more attention to data issues within governance and e-governance initiatives

— Funding and facilitating initiatives in the pilot project organisations that take a data-focused approach.

Stage 4: Building E-Governance Pilot Projects

Target Deliverable: a set of functioning E-Governance Pilot Projects from which lessons can be learned. The emphasis on partnership and process means that e-governance priorities will be set mainly on a national basis. In particular, those priorities (and the speed of their implementation) will tend to follow the political 'fault-lines' within the elites of particular countries.

Nonetheless, some potential priority areas for specific e-governance projects can be suggested. Here, the focus will be on pilot projects within the overall area of 'Networked Government' as defined at the start of this chapter. These could be drawn from any sphere of e-administration, e-citizens, e-services and government-related e-society. From the donor side, it is possible that emphasis would be given to projects that support more general governance goals. Examples could include:

— *Making strategic connections in government:* strengthening the role of the legislature by providing Internet-enabled flows of information on public sector accounts, spending against target and other performance measures.

— *Talking to citizens:* addressing accountability by providing Web-based information on public service types, schedules, availability and entitlements; and on details of government budgets and expenditure. This would recognise that most information flow to citizens would be intermediated by NGOs and the like.

— *Improving public services:* setting up basic interactional Web sites that facilitate the informational components of public services; for example providing forms that can be downloaded and printed, or simple request/feedback forms. This stage would probably be divided into two components:

Identifying E-Governance Pilot Projects

This would be a negotiated activity between key stakeholders such as donors, national ministries and institutions of civil society. These negotiations could usefully be undertaken at the national Strategy-Making Workshops proposed earlier. National E-Governance Units would be likely to take the lead on project implementation. Donor/cross-national inputs could include:

- — Funding or co-funding for pilot projects.
- — Advisory inputs to support various stages of the project lifecycle, including monitoring and evaluation
- — Dissemination of best practice lessons from the pilots.
- — Advisory inputs on scaling-up through replication of successful pilot projects.

Focusing specifically on government, the benefits are that e-governance initiatives can:

- — cut costs,
- — speed up decision making and service delivery,
- — increase the capacity of government,
- — improve the quality of decision making and service delivery, and
- — enable innovative approaches to governance.

This, in turn, can have broader effects. First, by improving the work of government, you improve the lives of all those businesses and citizens which interact with government. Second, by being catalytic. Within government itself, e-governance can catalyse cultural changes that improve governance.

In society more broadly, the presence of e-governance initiatives can be a national change catalyst in two ways: first by its demonstrator effect to other sectors; second, by building local ICT capacities. In India, for example, the decision under Rajiv Gandhi to press ahead with computerisation of passenger reservations on the railways had a major catalytic effect. It sent out ripples into both business and civil society that have helped put India where it is today in ICT terms.

Could the type of efficiency and effectiveness gains identified above be achieved without recourse to ICTs? In theory, perhaps they could. There are certainly good arguments for 'putting your house in order' by non-technology reforms prior to ICT use.

However, good governance requires an ever-increasing speed, volume, connectedness and complexity of information handling. The proportion of governance reforms that can be conducted without ICTs is therefore dwindling rapidly. Secondly, and still recognising the importance of an integrated approach, ICTs are a major tangible lever to change: they change attitudes, work pace, even whole work cultures in a way that earlier levers have not. If introduced according to the principles outlined above, they can therefore be highly cost effective.

Cost/benefit analysis is not a viable way to evaluate e-governance. Recent estimates suggest at least 80% of the costs of ICT-related projects are taken up in intangible, largely hidden costs. Likewise, the majority of e-governance benefits are also intangible.

Indeed, there is a strong argument for not making cost/benefit analysis the central plank of decision making. Where this has happened in Western government, not only are the figures involved spurious, but initiatives tend to be restricted to basic clerical automation, preventing real progress with e-government. In developing countries, where ICT costs can be 2-3 times higher while clerical costs are up to 10 times lower, even these basic projects would probably be struck out. Like it or not, one must take a leap of faith, an acceptance that e-governance is the future of governance and that we have to press ahead.

Developing country governments can either jump on and try to steer it as best they can. Or they can stand aside and watch other nations ride off into the future without them.

The overall impact can be described in terms of the deliverables outlined above for each stage earlier; that each developing country would gain:

— Awareness and commitment to e-governance at a high level.

— A set of key e-governance institutions that can strategically plan and facilitate e-governance projects.

— New laws and regulations that enable e-governance.

— A national E-Governance Strategy.

— The operational capacities to implement e-governance pilot projects.

— A set of e-governance pilot projects focused on 'networked government'.

All of these would serve to directly address key problems identified for e-governance development. They would thereby accelerate the move to good governance and e-governance in developing countries. Each component of the NeGI is associated with a target deliverable that can be turned into a measure. Some potential measures include:

— proportion of governance initiatives that contain ICT components,

— number of countries with: E-Governance Units; e-governance policies,

— proportion of e-governance initiatives that follow the principles outlined,

— proportion of e-governance initiatives that succeed, and/or

— number of e-governance initiatives undertaken within a country

Benefits achieved from e-governance initiatives could be included but, given the intangibility of many benefits, measures would be largely for presentational purposes only.

Political Acceptability

Despite the importance of technological and skill infrastructures, it is the politics of e-governance initiatives that probably hold the key. E-Governance projects have made slow progress in many countries because they do not serve the political self-interests of the major stakeholders, particular senior public officials.

The experience of India has shown that, where political leaders perceive they stand to gain from e-governance and support it, it moves on despite the other obstacles. Experience elsewhere has shown that, where stakeholders perceive they may stand to lose – or even merely to gain nothing – from e-governance and do not support it, it fails despite the presence of other success factors.

The views of senior public officials are therefore absolutely critical; hence the emphasis laid on the issues of leadership and commitment, the emphasis on building awareness and confidence, and the emphasis on 'winning hearts and minds'. Public officials must be convinced that e-governance is in their self-interest:

— in order to gain election victory,

— in order to respond to threats,

— in order to gain access to donor funds,

— in order to gain control, credibility, kudos, and other intangible resources, etc.

Other civil society stakeholders – managers, users, citizens in some cases – have less power but can still delay, skew or block e-governance initiatives. Building capacities, listening, addressing self-interest and motivation, and devising adequate incentives will all have a role to play here. Vendors have much to gain, but have the potential to skew initiatives unless they can be kept in check. Hence the importance of building up the 'intelligent customer' capacity.

Many developing countries do 'not have governance that even approximates to a normative framework. Many states lack stable polities; many lack macro-economic stability; in many, rule is by personalised leadership with rule by the executive that largely marginalises the legislature and judiciary; there are social cleavages along ethnic, tribal and other lines in many developing countries. Within this milieu, the potential for e-governance initiatives to make a significant difference may well be limited. However, that is not a rationale for inaction, and one must recognise that ICTs can act as a relatively concrete lever to change.

Sustainability

Where does the recurrent funding for e-governance come from when all the press photos have been taken and the donors/politicians have moved on? What happens when ministers and senior civil servants move on? These days you cannot find the elephants' graveyard because it is hidden behind the ICT projects' graveyard where the bleached boards of thousands of PCs lie rotting. Considerations of sustainability must therefore be high on the agenda in planning e-governance initiatives. Overambitious timescales lead to short cuts that reduce sustainability; for example bringing in expatriate consultants or looking for off-the-shelf ICTs. Adhering to the 'keep it simple' principle can help here. So too can making project scheduling more recipient-driven than donor-driven.

The danger of e-governance being too external: many e-governance initiatives in developing countries are donor- or vendor-led. The latter is particularly problematic given often conflicting objectives between vendors and governance, and the poor quality of some vendors. Care must be taken that both initiatives and institutions relating to NeGI do not become vendor-dominated.

The danger of e-governance being too internal: for some ruling elites in developing countries, 'it seems that governance is seen as a tool for serving personal, then ethnic, then social affiliation and last the national interest. All state machinery, institutions and mechanisms are viewed and used in this light.' E-Governance initiatives will be just the same: if senior public officials do come to see e-governance as being in their interests and are able to take control of those initiatives, they are likely to steer projects towards their self-interest, and potentially away from broader goals. It is very difficult, but a balance must be struck between external and internal interests. One lesson from a recent Zambian MIS initiative was that an independent project team was required 'so that government cannot intimidate team members and that donor countries cannot hijack the project for their own benefit.'

Donor fadism

There is a danger that some donors too readily run away with the latest fads in ICTs and miss the hard grind of churning out vital but unsexy basic administrative and managerial information systems. When e-governance projects focus on Web sites, for example, who are these for: local people or Westerners? White elephant projects can be introduced before a critical mass of users exists. Such Units are not a panacea: they can be weak and find it hard to push initiatives through within individual ministries and agencies.

5

Information Systems and Government

Information and communication technologies do change the way communities view themselves; giving communities hope, acting as a tangible sign that external agencies are helping. Nevertheless, overarching community objectives do make sense as the starting point for ICT strategy, ensuring that ICTs are primarily seen as a means to community ends. Strategy can be structured around the notion of input-process-output-outcomes: inputs of ICTs and related inputs will, via various electronic delivery/digitisation processes, lead to outputs of digitised community information and services, leading to outcomes of improvements in various community economic and social indicators. In a way, this can be a kind of mission statement for the community informatics strategy.

IT can make to the relationship between local governments and the communities they serve: in 'grassrooting' government; in building social, political and economic coalitions; in building representation upwards and outwards; and in mobilising the bureaucracy. However, the potential of IT frequently remains just that: a potential that is not actualised. The application of IT in government is beset by both barriers and problematic outcomes.

Barriers to IT Applications

The barriers to IT implementation can be summarised in the form of a 'DEPREST' framework:

— Data and information barriers, such as those which prevent data being shared between different government departments.

— Emergencies, such as the current need to divert substantial efforts and resources into the 'millenium bug' problem; something that, once solved, will have cost billions and yet generally left government systems exactly where they started in functional terms.

— Political and legal barriers, such as the lack of an adequate legal infrastructure to deal with electronic commerce, trans-border data flows, electronic records keeping, and other issues of information age government.

— Resource barriers, particularly the barriers of human resources, since the absence of adequate numbers of capable staff has long beset the public sector.

— Economic barriers, which have pushed themselves further up the agenda of late with the reality of national and regional recession and the threat of global recession.

— Socio-cultural barriers, such as the 'bureaucratic mindset' that may see IT as a tool for government automation, but not as a tool for government transformation.

— Technological barriers, such as the difficulties of internetworking.

These barriers also contribute to negative outcomes when IT is applied in government. Richard Heeks provided a guesstimate that up to 80% of public sector IT applications can be regarded as failures, particularly if one extends failure to encompass not merely the total failure when no workable information system is produced, but also:

— *Partial failures*: when goals are unattained or there are undesirable outcomes.

— *Sustainability failures*: when a system works for a short while but is then abandoned, for example, when the donor agencies, organisational champions or consultants move on to fresh pastures.

— *Replication failures*: when a successful pilot system cannot be reproduced on a larger scale.

Piers Cain provided an example of such failure in describing the impact of automated systems on accountability and records keeping in government. This has, at times, led to a diminution of accountability since intangible computer-based records are far more malleable and less durable than paper-based records.

This was but one instance of three archetypes of IT, government and development failure that Richard Heeks described:

— *Rationality-reality gaps*: failures that arise from the formal, rational way in which information systems are conceived, which mismatches the informal, subjective, self-interested realities of many public sector organisations.

— *Private-public sector gaps*: failures that arise from application in public sector contexts of information systems developed for the private sector.

— *Country context gaps*: failures that arise from application in developing countries of information systems developed in Western nations.

In seeking to realise the potential of IT to support government's contribution to the development process, the starting point must be to look beyond the technology. At the workshop, four integrated starting points were identified in harnessing IT:

— *Aims and objectives*: IT is a means to achieving organisational aims and objectives, not an end in itself. Therefore recognition of those aims and objectives must be a starting point for IT application. David Newman therefore described a necessary focus in developing community networks in bridging the 'how to' gap: the gap between community/project objectives and the issue of how to apply IT to support those objectives.

— *Processes*: the organisational processes that achieve the organisation's objectives. Philip Veasey described the importance of processes and process models in application of IT. Indeed, there were suggestions from the presentations of both Piers Cain and Chipo Kanjo that a precursor to introduction of IT might well be the re-engineering of organisational processes. The danger, otherwise, is that automation of ineffective processes will leave the organisation with still-ineffective processes; only processes that are now more quickly, more expensively, and more voluminously ineffective than before.

— *People*: the human component of all organisational systems, including information systems, that is the key to performance. Any application of IT must comprehend this 'human component', building in a consideration of, for example, political/personal objectives and cultural values.

— *Information*: the foundation of all information systems, yet one that seems often ignored in the idolisation of technology. Shirin Madon described the value of focusing on information as a vital way to understand the relationship between citizens and government in development of the growing numbers of 'megacities' worldwide. Chipo Kanjo and her co-author David Mundy have been putting these ideas into operation in Malawi, through a learning-based approach that encourages public managers to think systemically, to identify their information needs, and to identify strategies to meet those information needs.

In summing up these ways forward, and as an antidote to the earlier DEPREST model, one may conclude that effective application of IT in government to support development must be HAPPI because it puts at its Heart: Aims, Processes, People, and Information.

Internet use of Gcvernments: A case study

The Government of Sweden has undertaken local government empowerment during the 1990s. There were high hopes that this could be supported by new information and communication technologies. With this in mind, the city of Gothenburg embarked on the DALI (Delivery and Access to Local Information and Services) project in the mid-1990s. DALI was intended to provide citizens with information about government services, and with an opportunity to understand and participate in policy debates. Three pilot districts in Gothenburg, each with around 15,000 inhabitants, were selected for the project. Four leading politicians on each district council were given a PC.

In addition to home/work access for citizens, a small number of public kiosks were provided. The DALI Web sites were created with:

— An administrative information section about availability of, and access to, council-provided services (though no facility for online application).

— A current issues section covering council policy proposals and news about council services.

— A debate forum for moderated debates on policy issues, such as road planning in the district, in which both citizens and politicians could participate. Politicians' email addresses were also provided.

— An archives section of past discussions and documents with a free-text search facility.

Evaluation reveals that the project has had only a modest impact and can only be termed a 'partial success'. District home pages register around 40 hits per day, and the total number of debate contributions per year has been just a few dozen, mostly from citizens and hardly at all from politicians. This result called for more detailed analysis through interviews with key stakeholders, which revealed a series of 'tension dimensions' around local government use of the Internet.

Tensions Over Access

Cost vs. Value: Internet access needs to be higher before debate and usage will reach any kind of self-reinforcing critical mass. Yet raising access levels either means waiting for technology diffusion or pushing it by investing scarce resources. Kiosks particularly were very costly to operate since a number were vandalised or accidentally damaged.

Politician vs. Citizen: Access where money is available for access-raising investments, there are difficult decisions to make between increasing the ability of politicians and the ability of citizens to participate in the project. Adopting a 'bit of both' strategy potentially leaves neither with critical mass.

Tensions Over Content

Local vs. Central Web Design Control: central (city- or national-level) control over Web design can provide benefits of consistency, scale economies, and a clear locus for learning. Local control offers the ability to customise to particular district requirements. There were continuous internal political wranglings about control.

Government vs. Other Information Content: some officials feel government-funded sites should contain only government-authorised, government-related information. Others want to make their home pages a one-stop site for everything going on within a given district, including information about local shops and business. The former view prevailed, but the latter would have brought a higher hit rate.

Privacy vs. Accessibility of Personal Details: in Sweden, two legal principles collide in putting government information on the net. On the one hand, citizens have a right of access to government documents; on the other, holding of personal details on computer, requires a special permit for each instance. Districts tend to escape the collision by the rather ungainly solution of removing names from online government documents, or by just not putting documents online.

Tensions Over Debate

Censorship vs. Openness: full participation and freedom of expression are generally encouraged. Yet the 'psychological distancing' that occurs with use of computer-mediated communication leads to expression of extreme views that can cause offence and can easily sidetrack or halt debates. Balancing these two is not easy.

Necessity vs. Hesitancy of Politician Involvement: for debate fora to be effective, politicians must be seen to be contributing and taking note of contributions. This often ran counter to politicians' concerns about committing themselves in public, about having to give instant responses, and about being pushed along by the potentially unrepresentative few who bother to take part in Internet-mediated debates.

Direct vs. Representative Democracy: it is not always clear where such debates are headed. Are they tweaks to our current system of representative democracy that merely provide an electronic equivalent of the politician's mailbag and the occasional political meeting? Or are they driving forward a new model of democracy that will ultimately 'disintermediate' the politicians out of existence?

Addressing Tensions

Three elements help address the tensions:

- *Time*: some (but not all) problems of access will diminish over time as ICTs diffuse.
- *Tactics*: management guidelines agreed between the key stakeholders need to be developed to cover issues of content and control.
- *Strategy*: over and above these guidelines there must be a strategy which is more than just the 'suck it and see' approach that has driven many pilot projects. This must identify the Internet merely as a tool to meet broader democratisation goals, ensuring that the 'technology tail' does not wag the 'democracy dog'.

Nevertheless, there is no simple resolution to the tensions described. Some of them will remain fundamental to Internet-enabled links between citizens and government, reminding us that the Internet is no 'magic bullet' to solve the problems of governance and democracy.

Evaluating Electronic Community Networks

In many parts of the UK, many people are setting up community networks that provide Internet services aimed at the community and voluntary sector. In Northern Ireland, there are over 5000 community and voluntary groups serving 1.25 million people. Electronic community networks here do not have to take on the double burden of organising community activities as well providing support through Information and Communications Technologies (ICT). So Northern Ireland is a good place to study how electronic community networks can deliver benefits to communities, through their own groups.

We evaluated two community networks at an early stage in their development. Community Information Network Northern Ireland (CINNI) was, at the time, providing Internet access to a little more than 100 groups. It was running on a trial basis sharing dial-up facilities with the NI Civil Service, while seeking funds for a full-scale launch.

Since this research was completed, it has achieved funding and been launched with the aim of connecting thousands of groups in Northern Ireland to the Internet. A smaller network has been set up to connect rural communities, the North Antrim Community Network (NACN). They have provided one computer and modem to each village, for use in local community development.

Much of the literature on community networks makes little attempt to evaluate their benefits. What evaluation there is has mostly been written from the viewpoint of the network organisers, not the people and organisations that use the network. We based our evaluation on the self-identified needs and wishes of the participating community and voluntary groups. We studied their goals, the constraints under which they were working, their current experiences, and their hopes for future uses of the Internet, using a range of research techniques.

We found quite a difference between what groups hoped to achieve by using the Internet, and the benefits they had achieved, with a corresponding lack of use of the community networks by many of the members. In most cases, this was not because of any problems in access or Internet awareness. The problem was that staff or volunteers in the groups did not know how to use the software and services to support their organisation's aims or their project's objectives-the "how-to gap". This has important implications for both users and providers of community networks.

The rapid urbanisation that is transforming the developing world is creating cities which on the one hand offer opportunities for global economic activity, but on the other hand are beset with serious local social problems such as the growth of slums and automobile pollution. This phenomenon of rapid urbanisation is posing challenges to planners in developing countries.

As it becomes harder and harder for planners to disentangle the global from the local, it is increasingly recognised that without a solid local base, city governments will not have the strength that is needed to participate in global economic activity. We argue that the establishment of a solid local base requires democratised political mechanisms based on administrative decentralisation and the participation of citizens in municipal management. At the heart of these new management processes are activities concerned with information provision.

Some computerised information systems (IS) do succeed in the public sector, but the vast majority - quite possibly at least 80% - fail in some way. To explain why this happens, and how failure rates may be reduced, this chapter describes an 'ITPOSMO' model of conception-reality gaps. This argues that the greater the gap between current realities and the design conceptions of a new information system, the greater the risk of IS failure.

Three archetypal large design-reality gaps affect the 'government and development' domain:

— *Rationality-reality gaps*: failures that arise from the formal, rational way in which IS are conceived, which mismatches the informal, subjective, self-interested realities of many public sector organisations.

— *Private-public sector gaps*: failures that arise from application in public sector contexts of IS developed for the private sector.

— *Country context gaps*: failures that arise from application in developing countries of IS developed in Western nations.

Some generic conclusions can be drawn about successful approaches to IS development, such as the need for context-specific customisation, and the need for information technology professionals to act as more broadly-based change agents. More specifically, techniques can be identified for each of the seven ITPOSMO dimensions that will help close the gap between conception and reality.

IT and Accountability

If 'electronic government' means anything, it means the use of IT to help deliver the goals of public sector reform. These goals can include decentralisation, higher quality public services and increased accountability that will make public servants more accountable for their decisions and actions. But can IT deliver on this last goal? There are many cases in which IT has helped.

In the UK, for example, IT-based systems have helped increase the accountability of new public agencies to their political masters in central government through improved reporting of expenditure. The same has also been true, say, in Tanzania, where IT-based systems have helped increase accountability of government departments to major external finance providers like the World Bank and the IMF.

Yet IT is not a necessary part of the accountability equation. The recent mass movements behind government accountability in India, for instance, have involved citizen meetings, typed reports and, at their most high-tech, the use of photocopiers - but not a computer in sight.

Because it is information, not technology, that is essential to accountability. Information about the performance of services and programmes, decisions and actions must flow from public servants to those who would hold them accountable. But these information flows do not have to be supported by IT.

When accountability information flows are supported by IT, problems sometimes arise.

First, because IT seems to be skewing the balance of public sector accountabilities. To understand this, we must first understand the accountabilities of public servants. The accountabilities include:

— Managerial accountability to senior public managers.

— Legal accountability to the judiciary.

— Professional accountability to peer group members.

— Public accountability to citizens and clients.

— Financial accountability to finance providers, such as central government or aid donors.

— Political accountability to politicians and the legislature.

In many cases, application of IT has not been equally divided between these various accountabilities. Instead, IT-based accountability systems have largely been funded by finance providers to support financial accountability. Public managers increasingly attend to these systems and, given their limited attention capacity, start to ignore their other accountabilities, especially public accountability. In sum, despite rhetoric that 'the citizen is king', IT is making public organisations more accountable to central government or to aid donors, and less accountable to the general public. Only a significant investment in electronic public accountability systems will redress this growing imbalance.

Though, the qualities of IT have a tendency to fundamentally undermine accountability. Where public managers lack a clear records management strategy, computerisation has often been associated with diminution or even loss of paper records-keeping. Yet computer records, because of their intangibility and malleability, are a far poorer basis for accountability than paper records.

'The medium is the message' and the message of electronic media is one of truth, objectivity and credibility. So, when often-inaccurate public sector data is produced by computerised accountability systems it gains a mask of objectivity and an aura of credibility that it does not deserve. Recipients can be led to believe in the validity of invalid accountability information, thus undermining the process of accountability.

The overall growth of 'electronic government' itself is problematic. As public sector computing spreads up and out from its original clerical automation applications, it will increasingly make an input to managerial decision-making. This leads to a confusion and undermining of accountability because - to the delight of lawyers worldwide - there is no clear answer to the question: "Who is to be held accountable when computerised information systems in the public sector are involved in decisions and subsequent actions that are judged to be sub-standard?"

IT may therefore support the accountability component of public sector reform, but it may equally skew or undermine it. So, if IT is no panacea for delivering on accountability, what factors are important? Two related factors can be identified.

The first is consensus among powerful stakeholders about the desirability of accountability. Take the example of a public sector railway system in Asia. Computerisation was to be introduced to increase the accountability of ticket sales. However, the powerful stakeholders - in this case stationmasters - desired an increase in the accountability of clerical staff but no increase in their own accountability. Computerisation was only able to proceed successfully once the system was redesigned to automate clerical procedures but to leave the activity of stationmasters untouched.

Electronic accountability initiatives (and, indeed, electronic government initiatives more broadly) must therefore start with stakeholder values, culture and self-interests. Where IT supports these interests, it is likely to succeed, albeit at a cost of delivering more limited organisational goals. Where IT conflicts with these interests, failure is the most likely outcome.

The second factor is the approach that public officials take to information age reform. We can characterise a 'four-eyes' model of different possible approaches:

— *Ignore*: Public officials are ignorant about IT and about information. They therefore do not include consideration of either in their plans for public sector reform.

— *Isolate*: Public officials remain computer-illiterate and lack an understanding of information's role. They nevertheless are aware of IT and its potential. Investment in IT is therefore included in reform plans - often as an afterthought - but is seen as the separate responsibility of 'IT experts'. It is not linked in any systematic way to the process of public sector reform.

— *Idolise*: Public officials have become semi-literate. They use computers and are over-aware of IT's potential. They believe that IT can transform the business of the public sector (or at least transform their own career prospects if they are seen to initiate a high-profile IT project). They are dimly aware that information is something important.

— *Integrate*: Public officials have become information-literate. They recognise information as a key organisational resource that is central to all public sector functions. IT is relegated to a secondary role: it is seen as a valuable means to achieve certain reform ends, not as an end in itself. The reengineering of information systems and the introduction of IT are now fully integrated into the process of organisational change, driven by reform objectives.

Many of the problems of accountability skews and undermining arise because officials adopt an 'isolate' or 'idolise' approach to this strand of information age reform. They must be educated to adopt an integrated approach which places the goal of accountability first, reengineered information flows second, and which removes any sense that computerisation per se is a goal of the public sector.

Combined with the issue of consensus, this produces a four-step approach:

— Acceptance by key stakeholders of the need for accountability reform.

— Identification and communication of an agenda for accountability reform.

— Identification of the new and/or reengineered information systems requirements of this accountability reform agenda.

— Identification of the role, if any, that information technology has to play in meeting these requirements.

Approaches to information systems management

Public sector IT managers face problems resolving the conflict between two approaches to information systems management:

— *Centralised*: where decisions are taken at the most senior or central level.

— *Decentralised*: where decisions are taken at some level lower than the most senior; typically by individual work units within the organisation or even by individual staff.

Senior public managers particularly like the promise of centralised approaches, which can bring benefits of:

— *Resource sharing*: especially the cross-organisation sharing of data, technology and staff.

— *Duplication avoidance*: since, for example, any item of data is stored once and only once.

— *Learning and control*: because these have a central organisational focus.

— *Scale economies*: for both external purchases (hardware, training) and internal processes (system development, management).

Notions of joined-up government have put centralised approaches firmly onto the public sector agenda, but barriers to centralisation are well-entrenched. They include:

— *Technical barriers*: that make interconnection between existing systems complex.

— *Resource barriers*: since centralised approaches require an overt, 'up-front' commitment of money, time, people, and skills; all of which are in short supply.

— *Political barriers*: that make public servants unwilling to let "our data" or "our systems" become "the organisation's data" or "the organisation's systems".

— *Structural barriers*: that prevent the different parts of the organisation working together. In addition to the structural 'stovepipes' that beset government, stereotypical structural chasms still persist between: top managers who fail to understand information and IT; IT staff who understand technology but not the organisation's business; computer illiterate staff who still feel threatened by new technology; and computer literate staff who want to pursue their own agenda without central interference.

Even if centralised management of information systems can be pushed through, it represents no panacea for government since it binds the public sector ever-tighter with thick 'electronic concrete'.

The result is more time-consuming decision-making on IT, inflexibility to meet the needs of users and of future environmental changes, and greater dependence and vulnerability.

Decentralised management, of course, promises to avoid such disadvantages. Driven on by ever-increasing performance/usability:price ratios being delivered to the desktop, this is in synchrony with the push for greater autonomy of work units and greater individual responsibility in the public sector.

It promises to deliver:

— *Greater fit between systems and local needs*: by reducing the 'distance' between users and IT managers.

— *Higher usage of computerised systems*: especially where end users make a significant contribution to system development.

— *Faster system development*: for the same reasons.

Yet, the decentralised approach too is hard to implement given heavy investments in existing central systems, the lack of skills to support decentralised approaches, and the (sometimes covert) antagonism of many senior staff. It can also be expensive and chaotic, leading to higher-than-desirable costs and a lower-than-desirable scope of public sector processes.

Both the centralised and the decentralised approach can provide benefits for public organisations. Yet, at the same time, such approaches can be hard or impossible to implement, and can produce serious disadvantages for the organisation. What is the way out of this quandary? One way forward is the adoption of a 'core-periphery approach' that attempts to reconcile the push of centralisation with the pull of decentralisation.

It does this in two ways. First, through integration: drawing the centralised and decentralised approaches together into some kind of unified or compromise approach. Second, and more commonly, through division. This accepts that both centralised and decentralised approaches will be found, and then attempts to set some demarcation lines that will keep the two separate, thereby allowing both to be accommodated.

A decentralised approach may be most economic for public organisations, because it saves on overt input costs. A centralised approach may be most efficient, because it avoids waste and duplication. But a successful core-periphery approach may be most effective, because it can simultaneously provide:

— the control necessary to share key resources (including data), to avoid duplication, and to achieve economies of scale; and

— the freedom necessary to meet user needs, and to overcome blocks to IT usage and IS development.

IS Planning

A core-periphery approach to IS planning involves strong and active participation of users and local units in the formulation of strategy. The planning process may then involve decisions about other elements of the core-periphery approach:

i) planning which data items are generic and which are specific;

ii) dividing out responsibilities for information systems development.

In line with other core-periphery elements, such plans may also aim to guide more than dictate.

A core-periphery approach may involve a separation of central and local responsibilities, as described below for areas such as data management and IS development. However, another strand can be an attempt to close the 'structural chasm' between staff identified above.

For example, there is likely to be some central IS (not IT) unit with a co-ordination role. It may have a management structure that involves end users and senior staff as well as IT staff.

It may be underpinned by a relatively open philosophy that looks outside the unit and genuinely regards the end users as its customers. It may seek to develop hybrid staff who understand both the context and work of a public sector organisation and the role, management and jargon of information systems.

A core-periphery approach to data management typically involves a division of responsibilities, as illustrated. This division defines the centre's role as being the management of 'generic' data items used across all or most of the organisation, such as employee, finance, project and service delivery data. The periphery's role would be to:

— make use of generic data,

— alter generic data only within certain centrally-determined limits, and

— control 'specific' data items used only by individuals or small groups.

Client/server - adopted by vast numbers of public sector organisations - is a classic core-periphery architecture, with its division of power and resources between the server core and the client periphery.

A core-periphery approach to systems development can involve a division of responsibilities. For example, it may define certain types of information system - mission-critical, cross-departmental, technically-complex - as suitable for central development. All others will be deemed suitable for decentralised/end-user development.

Core-periphery can also mean sharing or dividing responsibilities for development of an individual system between users and central IT staff.

A core-periphery approach to acquiring information technology typically involves a mixture of 'carrot and stick': encouraging users to follow standards, and providing some limited sanctions for those who do not. It also typically involves a flexible approach to standards that allows users some local leeway within a set of boundaries, possibly with 'opt-in' or 'opt-out' norms. Options include:

— reserving certain purchasing decisions for the centre, but decentralising the rest;

— limiting the size of decentralised IT budgets;

— setting central specifications but allowing free choice of model and supplier;

— setting organisational standards on a committee with strong user representation.

A common core-periphery approach is to centralise the planning of training for core information systems. Other training needs may be met, as requested, by end-user support centres or by informal training methods. There may also be central provision of access to open and flexible learning systems such as CD-ROM- or Internet/intranet-based training packages or videos.

Given the very specialist nature of many repair and maintenance tasks, there are very high costs in leaving them to individual end users. Many organisations, therefore, have at least one IT support employee per department who takes on this role.

Centralising this role even further can lead to response times and prioritisation that seem poor from a user perspective. However, the more specialised the role, the more the arguments for centralisation. Finally, though, one must recognise that decisions between centralised, decentralised, and core-periphery approaches do not just depend on objective rationality. Instead, they will be determined by an equation that includes:

— the current status of resources and organisational structures;

— past experience (good or bad) with one or other approach;

— external pressures;

— internal politics.

In the last case, senior managers often find themselves the ultimate arbiters between IT staff seeking centralisation and mainstream staff seeking decentralisation. Their innate preference may be for centralisation. However, in practice, the more senior managers can be open-minded about the issues described here, the greater the chance for an approach that is both feasible and beneficial for the organisation.

6

E-Governance in India

E-Governance might have caught the imagination of Indian governments only now but International Business Machines has been working with governments across the globe to bring in e-governance for years now. It has also set up an institute for E-Government in Washington D.C. In an exclusive interview with Prashanth Hebbar, IBM Global Government's Mark Cleverley elaborated on various aspects of E-Governance implementations.

Globally what is the experience with E-Governance implementations? Are governments coming back to you and saying, Yes this is good for us? Information technology has quickly become a major issue and an opportunity for most countries and regional and local governments. They are grappling with how to use IT to enable, stimulate and develop a more vibrant economy and improve government service. My conversations with governments around the world lead me to believe that the forces driving e-government can be categorised in the following way, which I call the drivers of e-government:

Services to Citizens and Businesses

— Improve customer satisfaction with access and response

— Achieve savings through moving services online

— Reduce burdens all round - queuing, travel, etc

— Internal Cost Efficiency and Effectiveness

— Make government employees more productive

— Share infrastructure costs with service delivery

— Improve process and cycle time

Economic Development

— Compete to attract investment

— Reduce burdens on businesses

— Enable businesses for the digital economy

— Create employment

— Develop existing workforce and attract new

e-Communities

— Enable virtual citizen and business communities

— Add at marginal cost over service infrastructure

— Contributor (quality of life) to economic development

Digital Democracy

Support e-mediated exchanges of value in democratic

process Information, opinion, campaigning, contributions, voting74% of surveyed European politicians saw strength in this area.

— Information gathering and analysis

— Assimilation and decision support

Each government contemplating an e-government initiative will probably have one or more of these areas at the top of its agenda. Many governments have published broad visions of how they plan to become an e-government: these visions stress a range of benefits from improved service and reduced costs, to improving economic competitiveness, to electronically connecting the community and laying the framework for a digital democracy. Much of the initial activity in government is being driven from within individual agencies as they put information and transactions online for citizens and businesses to access over the internet.

In general, governments are strongly supporting e-government initiatives and this is typical around the world and at different levels of government: national, regional and local. Most information from our customers and from independent assessments (consultants, etc) suggests that the pace of e-government will quicken over the coming years, and the breadth of government activity susceptible to e-government initiatives of various kinds will increase.

The number of private sector companies moving into the e-government market is in itself an act of belief that e-government will develop and bring the benefits of the digital age into the business of government itself.

This is supported by surveys that show the intentions of government itself - for example in their own plans to bring government services online. Many countries have set specific dates by which they intend to achieve e-government goals. While suggesting E-Governance implementations do you draw up a complete blue print and suggest radical changes in the way governments work or do you approach the implementation "project by project" model. This is highly dependent on the individual situation in which we engage. Some of our customers are more advanced, for example in the areas of infrastructure and of legislation and policy to support new requirements. In general, however, governments rarely change quickly in radical ways- and that is a positive thing, in that governments tend to test innovations thoroughly before adopting them. This means that we recognize the differences that exist in government and respect them when consulting on innovation and change in technology.

Typically that means that change is progressive, phased, based on strategy, vision, goal-setting, project definition, pilot, feedback, implementation, etc. Our approach to e-business in general is to enable for our customers a virtuous circle of

Build: Establish a blueprint for creating applications

Run: Provide a scaleable, available and secure operations environment

Transform: Enable the organisation to re-engineer process, structure and culture to achieve the benefits offered by the technology possibilities.

Leverage: Capture and apply knowledge within the organisation.

This cycle is the foundation of our application framework for e-business, which extends to encompass e-government.

Is there a working benchmark for good E-Governance?

There is a significant amount of research, experience and guidance available in the e-government area from a variety of sources. IBM has formulated from its own experience a set of offerings in e-government which range from visioning, strategy development, process change, service and application selection, through to implementation.

These offerings can be used to assist government customers to formulate their own strategy and activity plans. Our knowledge and experience across government activity around the world makes us particularly well-placed to help to "benchmark" - in the sense of understanding, presenting, and helping to implement global best practice in government organisations.

Can there be any standardization in E-Governance implementations across the globe? Standardisation can mean several things.

It is clear that a good degree of technology standardisation is going on, based on the internet and programming and data standards. We support and promote the most open standards in architecture and implementation - CORBA, Java, XML, etc. This lays strong and flexible foundations for deployment of new initiatives over time.

Standardisation of what governments do, in what sequence, to get to e-government, is becoming clear but more slowly. This is largely because, while governments tend to do the same fundamental things, the relative priorities and the way these things are done differs strongly by government and by level of government.

However, currently, at all levels of government and in most geographies, we see most activity in the establishment of an online channel for government services. This is often an early step, since it is visible, has high impact, and can be done in a relatively low-risk manner. We also see governments continuing to undertake traditional large modernisation programs for major functional areas such as tax, fiscal management, social services, public safety and justice. We see good communications taking place among governments about what e-government means and how to approach it. This is useful since it helps to share experiences and to focus on what can be achieved. It may be that over time this does lead to a generally accepted model of how you go into e-government.

There seems to be nothing but islands of E-Governance implementations across the globe. With such gaps can one see a coherent E-Governance implementation? Without strong senior political and operational leadership, most governments are slow to do the re-engineering that will be required to redesign processes and fully integrate the internet and e-government approaches into their operations. Resistance to change in government can sometimes be high and the features of e-government in particular can often challenge traditional regulatory and control functions.

E-government is a journey, not a destination. To take the first steps, of putting information and less complex services online, are relatively well understood and can be done quickly. However, moving to an integrated e-government, where the government has transformed its interaction with its constituents to become more customer-centric, outwardly focused, and service-oriented, is a tough step for most governments.

Most places today actually are at the "islands of e-government" stage. Moving beyond that will require significant commitment and leadership. The issues will be largely not technical - rather, they will be in the areas of process, culture and organisation.

What model do you think is ideal in a country like India for implementing E-Governance? Governments play three key roles in the broader e-business world:

— formulating policy and the legal framework for e-business

— providing investments and incentives to facilitate citizen and business participation in e-business

— using e-business to change the way they operate internally and externally

Therefore there are imperatives in each of these areas that India will need to undertake (and is probably undertaking today).

In implementing the third imperative - relating most specifically to the business of government itself - India, like any nation proposing to move into e-government, will face challenges that pertain to its individual government culture, organisation, processes, and technology.

In addition there will be specific issues for India relating to its demography and geography. The size of the country and the population make it challenging to formulate a single approach. With this in mind a distributed approach, based on city clusters or regions, may turn out to be the most effective governance model for e-government initiatives. This could allow different formats, approaches, business models (government-funded or involving private sector organisations), etc.

Some guideline areas that India's e-government strategy may need to encompass:

— Early (and enough) time spent on the strategy formulation and identification and mitigation of risk. (Gartner suggests that a large proportion of "e-business" projects fail for lack of some elements of this strategic and other planning).

— Portal technologies to provide the foundation for constituent interaction of the future Wireless technologies to address the potential problems of communications infrastructure

— Pervasive computing to provide different forms of access to a community which varies significantly by economic position, language preference, technology familiarity, etc.

— Education and marketing of the new approach to government/constituent interaction.

— Facilitation of service provision at all levels of government within a large, complex civil service organisation.

— Innovative ways to contribute to the funding of the e-government solution(s) that may be prioritised

Does IBM provide any forum for government officials and politicians to learn about E-Governance and interact with their counterparts? IBM has for many years been a significant thought-leader in the application of technology in government. We continue that role strongly today in the era of e-government, and a good example is the IBM Institute of Electronic Government, at our Public Sector Briefing Centre in Washington, D.C.

This facility showcases innovative e-government approaches and solutions from around the world and allows government leaders to develop their understanding of the possibilities and the approaches that will best support their needs. We also offer senior leaders both specific briefings and general showcases at which they can interact with their counterparts from other nations. The IEG also works with and sponsors work from academia and other organisations that researches aspects of the future of government. An example of the outcomes of this research is the Digital Readiness Review program, which can be used to assess a nation or a region's preparedness to participate effectively in the new digital economy.

Has IBM lined up any specific implementations for the government sector?

IBM has been involved with information technology in government since its inception. We have a superb track record of delivering technology products and projects in government. In the last five to seven years, over which time e-government has developed as a topic, we have established perhaps the broadest and most varied portfolio of e-government solutions and capabilities offered anywhere. It addresses the range of requirements from web enabling legacy systems, through providing "single-agency" transaction systems over the web, to integrating data and workflow across different parts of government. We also offer government consulting services covering e-government strategy through to implementation.

We have a broad range of offerings and capabilities along with significant experience both internally and with customers that accelerate the implementation of any facet of e-government. We have a wide range of agency applications that can be implemented quickly to produce immediate results. We also have a consulting methodology that can help senior government officials define a long term plan, select high impact areas for integrated solutions and determine the best way to create the infrastructure to support the plan. These approaches can be used separately and in parallel. Governments can move rapidly into the e-government environment by taking advantage of IBMs experience, offerings and solutions in the following areas·

Government consulting: and thought leadership on transformation and business process re-engineering combined with deep domain knowledge and e-business know-how in designing information to develop the plan for managing the e-government transformation.

e-business applications and integrated solutions that start with Web-enabled applications that can be incorporated into an open integrated framework for business areas such as revenue and fiscal management, social and human services, postal and public safety and justice. The frameworks incorporate technologies for managing customer relationships, optimizing supply chains, and creating enterprise resource management systems.

Services to build, integrate, or run government applications or IT infrastructures securely, proficiently and competitively and to evolve them continuously over time, freeing resources for more focus on core objectives.

Technology and infrastructure: to support government strategies in virtually all areas, from defense to research.

— Software (middleware) to centralize management and leverage large, complex, heterogeneous distributed networks.

— Scaleable servers to host large databases and high, unpredictable transaction volumes.

— Pervasive computing to enable mobile workers and to address the question of access for all (the "digital divide").

— Deep Computing for research and simulation in human genome/medical discovery, weather forecasting, fraud detection and abuse, nuclear weapon stewardship, and national security.

— Emerging standards to continue to enable growth - Internet2, XML, Java. Integration

IBM's IT industry leadership and our Government Relations teams around the world, to support legislative or policy change that is mutually beneficial to government and industry, when appropriate.

Leading the e-business transformation: The CEOs of governments need to take the same role as CEOs of companies in leading and developing the strategy and approach to becoming an e-government. A vision may set the stage, but government leaders must be proactive at forcing senior managers to identify key process changes that will have the most impact and then working cross agency to design and implement changes.

Creating a supportive policy: (i.e. legal and regulatory) environment for the necessary transformation and re-engineering of organizations and processes leading to e-government. This often requires forming alliances and partnerships with other parts of government, industry, or constituents.

Building strategies to compete: for corporate investments or jobs, not based on traditional incentives such as physical infrastructure or taxation environment, but on e-business capabilities and readiness. Governments should ensure the existence of a competitive infrastructure (from schools to the information highway) and look for ways to help businesses, particularly small ones, understand the complexities of the international marketplace. Governments can also work with the private sector to bring about a more competitive business community (e. g., traditional government procurement cycles and purchasing processes cannot be effective where Web years are three months long) and take steps to make the work force and citizens more internet savvy.

Leveraging the size and influence of government: as a buyer/user of IT to improve efficiencies, reduce costs, and in certain cases to incent industry to address unique requirements.

Seven years of Internet in India

Even in the seventh year of Internet in India, we have a poor track record to show to the world. What went wrong? In this exclusive article for CIOL, Zee Networks director, technology, Amitabh Kumar opines that India failed to implement the pragmatic policies it drafted.

Kumar, who made significant contributions towards introducing Internet in India in the late 90s, also feels that authorities failed to recognize the adverse effects of incumbent monopoly.

Seven years of Internet in India were completed on 15 Aug 2002, a date, which went largely unnoticed. In this period India has notched up around 5 million Internet users through 1.5 million net connections, a number far below the initial hopes of an explosive growth of Internet in India. Aug 2002, the world had reached 553 million Internet users with USA alone accounting for 166 million (30%) (Nielson Net reports) followed by Europe (24%) and Asia Pacific 14%. India accounted for just 5 million or barely 1% of the world users of Internet, a 0.5 % penetration in the country. Worse, it had no broadband sector of any significant size to speak of.

Pragmatic Policies

The Indian Internet had started with a great promise. The policy makers did not fail to recognize the potential of the net for a quantum group in the knowledge-based economy. The ISP policy of the Department of Telecommunications (DOT) was very pragmatic with free licensing to ISPs. India was one of the few countries to enact the *Information Technology Act 2000* to enable Digital signatures and e-commerce. Setting up of gateways for Internet, laying of fibers & cables was freely permitted to the ISPs. Tax incentives were showered on the industry, infrastructure status given & mergers and acquisitions facilitated.

Unfortunately the result is not in line with expectations of what has happened elsewhere in the world. The net users still stagnated at 5 million, less than India's 7 million mobile phones and less than 12% of the 42 million telephone connections in India. What went wrong in India which did not go wrong in the other countries?

Correlation of Internet vs. Penetration

Country	*Access cost (% of GDP per capita)*	*Internet users per '000*
India	16.82	5
Brazil	5.26	35
South Africa	5.26	34
Mexico	5.17	23
Malaysia	4.85	90
Thailand	4.02	74
Argentina	3.20	53
Italy	2.02	191
Spain	1.65	175
S. Korea	1.50	349
Germany	1.30	313
Australia	1.14	258
France	1.03	183
United Kingdom	0.91	554
Hong Kong SAR	0.84	542
Singapore	0.84	302
Canada	0.77	450
Denmark	0.71	296
United States	0.65	536
Japan	0.49	174
Sweden	0.12	506

With all the pragmatic policies, the makers failed to follow these through to the implementation stage. They failed to recognize the daunting role which incumbent operators have played worldwide to make telecom reform difficult to accomplish. In India the usage charges of Internet remain one of the highest in the world. Internet dial up is still charged as local calls, netting approximately Rs.26 per hour to the BSNL/ MTNL. Add to it the ISP charge of Rs.10 per hour. A typical household with 3 hours of Internet access per day would need nearly 3500 per month to have access to the net. *In fact just 20 hours of monthly net access in India costs 16.8% of GDP per capita.* This one of the highest in the world and compares to 0.12% in Sweden,0.65% in USA, 0.84% in Hong Kong, countries where net access has really taken off.

Correlation of cost of internet vs penetration

The DOT (now BSNL) as incumbent operator did not relent to reduce the charges for local access to the net. Elsewhere in the world, dial up net access began to be offered at flat rates (including dial up charges) of $10-15 per month (USA) & $15 per month (UK) and at similar rates elsewhere. DSL access averaged $40-50 per month.

Basic operators worldwide encouraged volume calling by offering reducing rates, and even offering shares of revenues to callers. Some of the basic operators in India also offered reduced local rates for Internet access. However, the incumbent BSNL in India thwarted every effort to lose even a fraction of its revenue.

Broadband was a star performer with Worldwide Broadband Subscribers crossing 46 million in 2002,with

25.6 million being on DSL and 20 million on Cable. Asia has been a strong area of Broadband Internet growth, apart from USA and accounted for 42% share of World's DSL market as per figures released by the DSL forum in Aug 2002. In South Korea, DSL is now operating on 26% of all installed phone lines.

70% of Hong Kong users have broadband access at homes. Even in USA, with much sparser urban density, broadband has reached 17% penetration. Broadband, via either DSL or Cable remains one of the fastest growing modes of net access. The growth in broadband net access exceeded 50% over the last year, despite a severe economic slump. There were many enabling factors. For example, in USA, the Baby Bells were, by regulation (Telecommunication Act of 1996) required to offer Unbundled Network Elements (UNE) i.e. any piece of their network could be hired by the competitive operators. DSL operators were therefore able to get local copper loops.

In 1998 this type of unbundling fever spread across Asia and Europe. Partially unbundled local loops (i.e. DSL/ADSL) have been made available in Asian markets like Japan, Hong Kong Australia & Singapore. Admittedly some of them have not made much headway yet due to high access charges, but the growth where it has happened is startling. For example in South Korea, the number of internet users leapt from 3.4 million in Feb 1999 to 15 million in May 2000- a four fold growth in a period of just 15 months.

In India nothing of the kind happened with all the copper loops being controlled by BSNL. In the absence of any regulation for offering lines to competitors, no such initiatives took off in India. Except for a couple of hardy operators no one could extract the concessions of local loops in return for additional revenue to BSNL. It is now, only on 23rd Aug 2002 that he BSNL has came out with a scheme of franchising the local loops for DSL type services at unsustainable rates of revenues share with no costs to be borne by them. However the services will remain that of BSNL. Bharti, a basic operator has now launched its Broadband DSL offering in India signifying the end of the virtual monopoly of the incumbent.

Broadband cable Internet has been one of the success stories in the US, primarily due to the high quality HFC and fibre network. Telephony over cable has been one of the drivers of net access over cable, whether switched, packet mode or as pure Internet Telephony. Internet telephony accounts for nearly 11% of the global International traffic today.

In India the regulations for net telephony were drafted heavily biased towards the Incumbent. First of all no Internet telephony operator can provide Internet phone service within India. In fact no connection to the phone network within India is permitted at all. So if a user buys a "Valufon" or "Bol Anmol" Card, he still can't call Bombay to Delhi.

For cable Internet it is a death knell. Reaching over 38 million homes many of which do not have a primary fixed line phone, it could have provided a cheap phone facility. However, this option is unattractive if a cable phone customer cannot call any one in India-not even emergency services.

With Compulsory Conditional Access (CAS) set to become mandatory, under the Ministry of Information and Broadcasting Initiative, a set top box will soon find a place in a majority of homes. An Internet phone, which can come virtually free with it will not however be possible- you can't call anyone in India – do no local shopping. The Incumbent BSNL & MTNL have ensured that their turf is protected at all costs. You can however call overseas (with VSNL being divested, the incumbency factor had vanished).

Internet Backbones

In the initial Internet years, USA constituted the hub of Internet and all other operators from Europe, Asia & Australia had to connect to USA in a Hub & spoke arrangement, paying both-way charges for all connectivity to US. It was expected that with the high growth rates being experienced in E·ırope and Asia, these would develop into Regional Hubs and US centric Internet would cease to exist. This however, could not be accomplished, though regional exchanges did come into existence. Due to the high leased line charges in India, backbones of Internet practically did not exist. National Long Distance operators (NDLOs) only could have provided backbones in India. The long distance policy brought into play in 2001 was apparently only to satisfy India's obligations under WTO and not to usher in serious competition to the Incumbent BSNL. To protect the turf of the incumbency provisions such as Rs.5 billion entry fee ($100 million) and compulsory roll out obligations for the entire country were put into place. The result: Only three operators even applied for the NLD license. The charges across the country for E1 range at Rs.2.2 millon per annum not counting the local loop. Even inter-city connectivity of 100 km costs Rs.500,000 ($10500) as per TRAI rates.

When the operators dropped the tariffs for long distance calls in India – they did not bother to reduce the leased line rates either local,or domestic reflecting the operation of a cosy system. The result: No backbones of Internet in India, fragmented networks & high operational cost for ISPs remains the stark realty today.

There were some views that other extraneous factors are inhibiting the growth of the net in India e.g. the number of PCs and lack of infrastructure. However, this is only partially true. India has over 7 million PCs with 1.7 million being added every year. The cost of PC hardware has fallen to a fraction of what it was seven years ago.

It is not these factors but the environment imposed by the incumbent BSNL - high dial up charges, high cost of backbone capacity denial of network elements such as local loops, which have bottled the growth of the net in this country. The result : Internet business became so bad in India that may companies simply wrote off their dial up & DSL businesses. The number of ISPs halved in India in 2002 while the International Bandwidth used by Internet Service Providers (ISPs) fell to 600 Mbps against 900 Mbps in 2001 as per the ISPAI. (ISP Association of India). Other service providers are really on thin ice, mostly awaiting regulatory or operating concessions to make a good business of a service which has done very well elsewhere. There can still be hope for the Indian Internet. Most projections for the Indian Internet continue to be very optimistic. As per IDC forecast, the number of net users will grow to 37.5 million by 2005.

This will however require more than a cosmetic change in the operating scenario. A global scale Indian Internet can be a reality only if the costs are kept down to affordable levels. Enabling regulation needs to recognize the need of competitive operators using infrastructure of the incumbent through unbundled network elements and follow through with policies which have been enacted over four years ago elsewhere.

The regulations also need to recognize the synergies in businesses such as internet and telecom, content and broadcasting. There is a need to eliminate the Chinese walls that prevent infrastructure created from being freely used.

CIOL Services

India aims to achieve an Internet subscriber base of 230 lakh by the end of 10th Five Year Plan. However, several vexed issues remain for the industry to pick up. ISPAI, the mouthpiece of the ISPs, is taking these issues up with relevant authorities to help ISPs come out of the loss-making mode, which is important for Internet usage to increase in the country. CIOL Bureau discusses these issues and the future of the Indian Internet industry with ISPAI general secretary Amitabh Singhal. Some key aspects that we need to address from the regulatory point of view are:

a) Bringing down cost of access to Internet by users, say the telephone charges

b) Time taken to get clearances for use of radio frequencies for last mile access

c) Proper interconnectivity regime between telecom companies and ISPs

d) Bulk rates/revenue sharing between telecom companies and ISPs

e) Addressing the gray market in Internet telephony, which has a very significant impact on ISPs

f) Cost of bandwidth, impacting significantly the financial viability of ISPs, etc.

Apart from the above, there are vexing taxation issues that we need to concentrate on. ISPAI is in touch with relevant authorities to sensitize them on the need to address such issues, so that the country's objective of achieving 230 lakh Internet connections during the 10th Five Year plan can be achieved. Most ISPs have recorded fall in their Internet subscriber base early this year. What are the main reasons behind it?

It may not be correct to generalize that most individual ISPs have recorded a fall in their subscribers. The truth is that only in couple of instances, the free subscription model failed due to which the total number of Internet subscribers was negatively impacted. While, as of March 2002, the total base was pegged close to 4 million, it was soon corrected to 3.3 million. Nearly 0.7 million free subscribers were taken out of the statistical figures as they are no more regarded as subscribers any ISP. Therefore, it would be more apt to say that there has been drastic fall in the growth rate, coming down from a high of over 200 per cent to just about 8 per cent per annum.

What are the main reasons for Internet to grow at a slow pace in the first seven years in India? Between 1995 up to end 1998, Internet services were a monopoly and hence the growth was miniscule. The total subscriber base during those years peaked at about 200,000. Beginning 1999, when the sector was opened up for free competition, it saw a very satisfactory growth rate of about 54 per cent per quarter in terms of subscriber numbers. The pace has slowed down considerably since mid 2001, which coincided with the universal dotcom bust. That however may have had a marginal impact maybe in terms of decreased investor interest in Internet and related businesses. One study conducted by ISPAI has enumerated the following barriers responsible for the current slow pace.

— Lack of PC penetration, as it is the most common device for accessing Internet

— Lack of relevant telecom facilities in non-metro areas, thereby restricting scope for expansion

— Cost of Internet access, i.e. dial up charges, as majority use this method

— Slow take off of technologies such as DSL, Cable Internet, etc.

— Limited availability of relevant content in local languages - eGovernance and eCommerce, therefore, are limited options

— Financial viability of service providers a question mark, effecting expansion plans

— Bandwidth costs are high and not in sync with international trends

— Co-operative efforts between telecom companies and ISPs yet to mature, so that market growth can be jointly worked at.

By when do you expect the ISP players to become profitable? What is the rough estimate of Internet subscribers that India should have for the ISPs to be profitable?

ISPs will become profitable once the subsidy that they provide to their individual customers goes away. (This subsidy is a leftover legacy from the dotcom boom era, when advertisement revenue was major buzzword.) ISPs revenue from subscription needs to become realistic. For that to happen, the current rates/charges have to go up. But on the other hand, the costs to provide the services need to be brought down.

The important part therefore is to not only have the critical mass of customers, but also arrive at the most efficient break-even point. There are various categories of service providers and it is up to them to decide their own critical mass depending on the scale of their operations and investments. Some ISPs are believed to be reporting operating profits, but wiping out accumulated losses is another task, which will take some time. As for the country, the task is clear cut, the Planning Commission has set a target of achieving 230 lakh connections for the period up to 2007.

What is the total bandwidth used for Internet traffic from India today? How much is it expected to grow in the next one-to-two years? The estimated usage of International bandwidth is in the range of 1-1.2 Gbps and may grow at a 25 per cent clip at the minimum, considering that there will be subscriber growth, Internet telephony will grow and ITeS services such as Call centers etc. will aggressively use internet. While ISPs claim to have more bandwidth than required by their subscribers, Internet connection is often choking during peak hours. Why is it so? Is there is mismatch between bandwidth claim and reality? There could be variety of reasons for choking other than just tall claims. It's in the way Internet works. The choke could be at any point in the transmission links running around the globe, at the service provider level, at the last mile, or there could be a problem at the any of the servers around the world from where information is accessed.

However, in India, TRAI, the telecom regulator has laid down certain Quality of Service (QoS) parameters, which once adopted, may to some extent perhaps improve the situation. However, it would still not be fail-proof. Poor connectivity has also adversely effected Internet telephony to become more popular. How do you see the future of Internet telephony?

India has a unique set of regulations for Internet telephony. One cannot use it for domestic long distance calls, which does restrict the potential quite significantly. As I explained in the earlier answer, the quality of net telephony is analogous to the quality of Internet access available at any point of time. Sometimes good sometimes not so good. Poor connectivity restricts proper use of Internet and by inference any application over it including telephony.

However, that holds good for telephony over the public Internet. In a managed IP network situation, the quality of telephony can be of level 4 (PSTN is considered level 5) and this is where service providers need to concentrate on for growth. Corporates and businesses are waiting to be tapped with 'cost effective' VoIP solutions. One critical situation that ISPAI is trying to find a solution to is the illegal market of Internet telephony. It is estimated that 70-80 per cent of the market is being eaten away by illegal players who are palming of cheap Internet telephony cards at the cost of genuine licensed service providers. What new options do ISPs have to increase their revenues?

ISPs for some time have been refocusing and rearranging their business plans. Increasing ARPU (average revenue per user) is the most obvious thing to concentrate on. Quality of customers and not just numbers, that's now becoming important. There has been a growing trend to provide various solutions, including consulting, co-location and hosting facilities to the corporate and business sectors, which provides for positive revenue generation.

Do you see Internet tariff going up in the near future? If yes, when and by how much? To some extent yes, the tariffs are seeing an upward trend and it's necessary to the extent that cuts the levels of existing subsidy and stem the financial bleed that ISPs have been facing. To enumerate, a study that was undertaken sometime back showed that on an average, it cost about Rs 15-16 to the ISP to provide an hour of access to the subscriber. At that time the average rates being charged were just about Rs 5-6 per hour.

Currently, the average charges are around Rs 9-10 per hour. However, it does not really mean that rates have to necessarily go up by another Rs 6. If we're able to reduce the cost of operations, say by way of reduced bandwidth costs and bringing in some more efficiency of network utilization, maybe only some marginal increase would do the trick of reaching the break even point. So there are different factors to be considered, taken into account and implemented upon before we can suggest any particular price point as optimal. What is the Internet? A global interconnection of networks enabling one to access any person, content or service that has an online presence or address. A medium that can carry data, content, voice or video, depending on the bandwidth available, enabling flexibility of use, diverse applications and services. The more utilitarian these are, the more it will be used.

But the Internet isn't just about email, messaging and chat. It is the single biggest opportunity India has had to build dominance in the delivery of online services worldwide. By leveraging India's advantage in knowledge resources. IT enabled services are growing at a rate of 65-70 per cent per annum and is expected to earn Rs 7,100 crores in 2001-02. And, it will continue to grow at this rate for the next three years, creating a million new jobs, as per the Nasscom-McKinsey study. The key to expanding this business opportunity for the country lies in making the Internet ubiquitous and affordable to all. For the rapid adoption of the Net as a business and personal enhancement tool, with a rapid learning curve resulting in many more companies investing in IT enabled services. Then the Internet will truly become a tool for giving India a competitive edge in global eCommerce.

Indian citizens will use the Internet for the benefits it affords them in daily life as more services come online. These need not be for the urban, sophisticated users alone. In a village near Pondicherry, a volunteer uses an Internet link-up to read weather forecasts and broadcasts them over a loudspeaker. For the fishermen who go out every day on frail wooden boats, knowing that a storm is approaching can mean the difference between life and death. They can now even download satellite images revealing where fish shoals are. The Internet also tells them the prevailing market price that day for their catch, helping them get better terms with bulk buyers. In the Gyandoot project of Dhar district, Madhya Pradesh , a collection of tele-kiosks run by local operators offer e-government services to citizens. The grievance system, a facility for citizens to lodge complaints against the government with a guaranteed response within one week, was one of the most popular information services of the program.

Making the Internet available as a knowledge resource to every Indian does not mean trying to provide broadband access to every village. Instead, providing a farmer with access to land records online is a tangible benefit: the Andhra Pradesh government is attempting to do just that. So the Internet needs to be made available to rural communities with content that is relevant and useful to them. With technologies and business models that work in their societal setting.

The governments of Tamil Nadu and Andhra Pradesh are investing in networking their states to make eGovernance a reality for their citizens. Their plans also include providing connectivity to decentralise the location of businesses in IT enabled services and Business Process Outsourcing from the capital cities to a network of satellite towns.

India need government policies that encourage investment in infrastructure, free and fair competition, the growth of eGovernance and IT enabled services. High capacity bandwidth, both national and international, new technologies for the last mile, community access centres in rural areas like cyber cafes all need to be made available.

7

Internet and International Issues

The Internet is a dynamic new communications medium which has emerged at an astounding pace in recent years. The Internet, is one of many on-line services which offers a revolutionary means by which individuals and organisations can communicate, entertain, educate and inform.

There is no central control or ownership of the Internet and the functions performed by the participants in the on-line environment are not as fixed as in existing media publications and broadcasting models. Most significantly, a person from anywhere around the globe can create content and make it available on-line.

The Internet has enormous potential as a means to enhance the diversity of information and entertainment available to individuals and corporations around the world. Its relatively low barriers to entry, which are identical for both speakers and listeners, provides access to all who wish to participate in the medium, and even creates a relative parity among speakers. It has been described as 'the most participatory form of mass speech yet developed'.

However, along with the growth of these services, and a recognition of the enormous benefits which they can provide, concerns have been raised around the world about the impact of the Internet, particularly in terms of the content which can be provided and accessed on-line.

Some have argued that there is nothing that can be done to manage Internet content, whilst others state that the issues can only be tackled by international cooperation. In the meantime many countries have been investigating and/or implementing their own regulatory measures in relation to the Internet and other on-line services.

In January 1997 the United Nations Educational, Scientific and Cultural Organisation (UNESCO) commissioned a pilot study from the Australian Broadcasting Authority (ABA) on the Internet and International Regulatory Issues. The pilot study has four main objectives. The first is to examine the nature of the on-line environment.

The second is to identify some of the legal and ethical issues which arise in that environment, particularly as they relate to content.

The third objective is to collect comparative data on the approaches taken by four countries, namely Australia, Malaysia, Singapore and the United Kingdom in response to these issues.

The fourth objective is to discuss the feasibility of a larger comparative study which may be undertaken following consideration of the pilot study.

Countries Included in Pilot Study and Methodology

The countries selected for the pilot study are Australia, Malaysia, Singapore and the United Kingdom. These four countries were not intended to be representative in any way and are dealt with in alphabetical order in respect of the topics considered in the study. The four countries do not represent all the major geographic regions of the world nor of the range of national responses to concerns about on-line content. Rather they were selected for the following reasons.

- Given the short time frame for the pilot study, ie. approximately 10 weeks, the ABA was conscious of the availability of existing information and the ease of obtaining additional information on the regulatory responses to on-line services in the countries selected;
- The ABA was also conscious of choosing countries which already had proposed or introduced measures in place in relation to on-line content;
- It was considered useful to have at least one 'less developed' country in the pilot study to provide a comparison to responses in 'more developed' nations;
- The countries selected are located in three of the major geographic regions in the world - Asia, Europe and the Pacific.

It was considered that four countries was the maximum number that could be dealt with in the pilot study in the time available. The collection of information for the pilot study was largely undertaken using information available on the World Wide Web (www) and through library sources. Contact has been established with a number of relevant government agencies and experts in the four countries to inform them of the study and their comments on the material in the drafts in terms of accuracy and completeness are being sought.

The Nature Of The On-Line Environment

The Internet consists of a network of computer networks which span the world. The Internet was developed in the 1960's for military purposes, as a decentralised communications system which could survive damage to one part of the network. Decentralisation remains an important characteristic of the Internet.

By the 1970s, academics began to use the Internet as the computer networks which had emerged in universities were first linked with networks in other academic institutions and later to the Internet.

In recent years there has been a dramatic expansion in Internet usage around the globe with an equally dramatise increase in the amount and range of material available on-line. Part of the reason for the growth in Internet usage flows from the relatively low costs of participation relative to other media. The necessary equipment comprises a computer, a modem and access to a telephone line, the cost of which is not insignificant but which is within the reach of many individuals and organisations.

It is important to note that the Internet did not depend on commercial incentives for its growth. Rather it has developed essentially from a desire to share and obtain information, entertain, and communicate. Many Internet users view themselves as part of an 'Internet community'.

The on-line environment has now become a rapidly expanding international medium in which literally millions of users are providing and accessing content on a daily basis. For this reason the Internet offers unprecedented variety and quantity of content that is continuously changing as content is added, updated and moved around the world.

As no single entity controls the operation of the Internet or the material available on it, it is impossible to form a picture at any point in time of what exactly the Internet looks like, its size or the quality or quantity of content available. Content accessible on the Internet is stored in thousands of linked computers and is equally available by and from governments, corporations, interest groups, institutions and individuals from anywhere around the world. At present most of this content is provided free of charge. Whilst material can be accessed from any computer connected to the network, it is important to note that the content may be actually stored on a number of different computers or 'servers', which need not be in the same jurisdiction as the person accessing or creating the material.

Participants in the On-line Environment

In order to understand the nature of the Internet it is useful to identify the functions which are being performed by those who are participating in the medium. These functions include providing content, accessing content, connecting others to the network and/or providing the telecommunications infrastructure. However, it is important to recognise that, unlike traditional broadcasting and publication models where the roles of content providers, publishers and viewers tend to be fairly fixed, the activities being performed by a participant on the Internet often encompass more than one function and many participants perform different functions at different times.

Of all the functions being performed in the on-line environment the distinction between 'users' and 'content providers' may be the most blurred. This is because any person or organisation can access and/or add to content available at any time. For example, a person can read and send text to a newsgroup or mailing list, create a web site or browse and retrieve information, all of which may occur in the same Internet session. Accordingly, drawing a distinction between accessing content and providing content is more a theoretical construct that usefully describes the two separate functions, which are often performed by the same participant in the on-line environment.

However, for the purpose of the pilot study, the term 'user' is generally used to refer to a consumer of on-line services who accesses material available on-line, typically via a link with the network through a service provider. A 'content provider' is described as a person or organisation which provides content in the on-line environment. Content may comprise text, data, still graphics, audio, video, computer programs or a combination of all of these.

Organisations and individuals who provide access to on-line services to other users and content providers are referred to as 'service providers'. This incorporates those who merely provide access to the computer network which makes up the Internet, sometimes called 'access providers', as well as those who provide access along with additional services to their clients, such as assisting clients to transform content into an attractive format display on the world wide web, facilitating easy access to new and/or interesting sites and help desk facilities.

Service providers range in size from individuals to small businesses, universities, government corporations and multinational organisations with operations in several countries. Service providers usually provide their clients with 'space' to store content, such as web sites, on their computers, which are sometimes called 'servers'. This enables their clients to create and provide Internet content which can be accessed by other Internet users. Different service providers have different policies regarding the material which their clients provide and store on their servers. Some service providers requiring content providers to meet certain standards, whilst others do not wish to concern themselves with the nature of content at all.

Some service providers also temporarily store or 'cache' popular Internet content from remote computers onto their servers in order to facilitate faster and more efficient access to this material for their users. Service providers who provide access to the Internet operate as part of a network of computers. Accordingly, they enable users to access content contained on their own servers, as well as material held on the network of computers which make up the Internet, which may be stored on computers within the country in which the service providers operate, or on other computers around the world.

It is important to recognise that due to the vast amounts of Internet content which can be accessed from computers all around the world, along with the fact that Internet content is constantly changing, service providers are often not aware of, and are not in a position to be aware of, most of the material which can be accessed by those who use their service. Encryption transfers and the use of alternative routes and protocols further exacerbates this issue and renders the blocking of even those sites which have been identified extremely problematic.

The network infrastructure necessary to support on-line services in any country is usually provided by telecommunication carriers. In the pilot study the parties who provide this service are referred to as a network infrastructure providers. On-line service providers usually lease telephone and data line capacity directly from the network infrastructure providers, or from 'resellers'. In some cases, a corporation may perform two separate functions in the on-line environment so that they fall within the definition of both a network infrastructure providers and a service providers.

Potential Uses and Opportunities Presented by On-line Services

The potential uses and opportunities presented by the Internet for enhancing the way we communicate and access information, educational and entertainment resources appear to be unlimited. Some of the major modes of communication presently available on the Internet include e-mail, newsgroups, the World Wide Web, Internet Relay Chat, voice and teleconferencing facilities to name only a few. Each of these services can be used for a wide range of purposes and each uses its own set of technical protocols. Given the extremely dynamic nature of the Internet, it is highly likely that the range and nature of the services available throughout the medium will continue to develop at a rapid rate.

As a Means of Communication

From the time the Internet was first developed it has been used for virtually all forms of communication, from one-to-one communications to one-to-many communications. Forums also exist for group discussions in real time, as well as over time.

One of the main methods of communications is Electronic mail, or e-mail as it is widely known. E-mail allows users to send text messages and files to one another via personal computers. Its popularity stems from convenience, speed of delivery and low cost, as well as the capacity to reach millions of people throughout the world. In addition, the ability to transmit files of information in the form of documents, spreadsheets, graphics, sounds and computer programs as attachments to messages makes e-mail a powerful application. E-mail is increasingly being used as a mainstream form of communication for individuals, governments, educational bodies and industry.

E-mail messages are most often used for private communication, as they are addressed to an individual person or group of named individuals. In this respect, e-mail can perform a similar function to letters, faxes and telephone calls.

E-mail messages can also be sent to groups of people who are members of mailing lists. These lists are usually maintained on specific computers to which individuals can subscribe by submitting their e-mail addresses. While some mailing lists are not controlled in any way, others are supervised in that each message sent to the list is reviewed by a moderator who then decides whether to allow the message to be sent on to members. Similarly, the acceptance of new members to a list may be controlled by a moderator.

An e-mail can also serve as a form of identification when a person subscribes to additional services or seeks to access content from other computers.

However, it is important to note that e-mail addresses need not reflect the actual name of any given person or organisation and a person may have several e-mail addresses and/or use pseudonyms or aliases in their on-line communications. E-mail addresses can also be falsified.

Usenet 'newsgroups' are another popular mode of communication. The term 'newsgroups' generally refers to a world wide distributed system of discussion fora. Fora have been set up on virtually every topic imaginable and users whose service provider subscribes to a particular 'newsgroup' can access and participate in these open group discussions.

Messages are posted onto news servers which are distributed to other news servers around the world. Content providers may identify themselves or participate anonymously.

Content providers can also communicate with a wide audience by establishing a web site on which they can display text, graphics, or provide video, audio services and software.

The ability to use these modes of communication to reach a potentially international audience is one of the most important aspects of the Internet. It has the potential to enhance social and political participation of individuals and enable the exchange of ideas across geographic and political boundaries.

As an Educational Resource

The Internet's capacity as an educational and cultural resource is enormous. Via the Internet users can access data bases, texts, journals, articles, reports, state documents, encyclopedias and legislation which are held by public and university libraries, government departments and organisations around the world.

Many art galleries, museums and cultural institutions have also established web sites containing images and information about works in their collections, providing an enormous amount of musical, video and other audio material of educational value.

The Internet also enables researchers and students to communicate directly with others with similar interests around the world. For this reason the Internet has been an extremely important resource for a large number of educational organisations for over a decade and the use of on-line services is well-established in the university and research environments.

In recent years, other sectors of education including schools have begun to utilise on-line technologies to extend the reach and effectiveness of teachers' work in terms of curriculum development, delivery of material and provision of professional support and development services.

The Internet also offers new possibilities for 'open learning' and learning by distance education. This has enormous potential to increase access to educational facilities for those in rural or non-metropolitan communities. It also enables students to enrol in a course of study with educational institutions around the globe.

As a Source of Entertainment

The Internet has the potential to become an important source of entertainment for users world wide. Already vast numbers of computer games, on-line magazines, newspapers, video and audio services are available on the Internet. Whilst many users can entertain themselves for hours 'surfing the net' for information, images and discussions regarding matters of interest to them, it is also important to note that in recent times many existing content industries are starting to use the Internet to deliver traditional audio and video products. Although the bandwidth available in most countries currently precludes television broadcasts from easily being provided on-line, many predict that it is only a matter of time before full motion videos become widely available on the Internet.

Over the next few years it is anticipated that the Internet will increasingly become a major source of the type of entertainment products which are currently available on television, radio, video and CD-ROM. As more secure methods of collecting payment for services over the Internet become available, it is expected that the Internet will also provide a common medium by which entertainment products are purchased.

Some Ethical And Legal Challenges Arising In The On-Line Environment

The international, interactive and decentralised nature of the Internet and its potential for making available vast quantities of content to and from anywhere in the world give rise to a number of legal and ethical challenges. The following is not intended to be a complete discussion of all the issues which arise from the Internet, but an outline of some of those issues which create significant challenges, particularly in relation to content.

Access, Participation and Diversity

Any individual who has access to the Internet can participate in the many modes of communication which function in the on-line environment, expressing their views in the form of text, images, or sound and accessing the vast array of content provided by others. For this reason the Internet has enormous potential to create a dynamic international on-line community in which the relative parity amongst users enhances freedom of speech and cultural, social, political, religious and linguistic diversity. However, it is important to recognise the critical role which access and active participation will play in this equation.

Equitable access to the Internet remains a fundamental issue which will impact on the ability of individuals to participate in the benefits available through the Internet. This will be affected by the economic paradigms operating within both national and household frameworks. The nature of the available telecommunications infrastructure and the costs of connecting to the network, typically via a service provider, will also impact on the opportunities presented to any given individual. Accordingly, ensuring equity of access to on-line services is emerging as a major challenge which is likely to have a concomitant impact on the issue of access to information, educational facilities and cultural resources and all of the opportunities which flow from these.

It is also recognised that whilst the Internet provides the opportunity for immense diversity of content, at least at present, a significant proportion of Internet content appears to originate in Western liberal democracies, and particularly the United States. This material inevitably reflects some of the social, political and ethical values of those communities. A substantial proportion of Internet content is also only available in the English language.

One of the challenges if the Internet is to reach its potential as a diverse medium will be to ensure that it does not become an increasingly homogenised environment which enhances the dominance of particular languages and cultural perspectives. In this regard it is noted that many countries have adopted strategies for television and radio to ensure local content and community participation in those mediums. These strategies are not easily adopted or even appropriate for Internet communications.

In order to maximise the diverse content and range of cultural and linguistic perspectives which can be accessed on-line it will be important to not only maximise access to the Internet but also to encourage all participants in the on-line environment to play an interactive role and contribute to the body of data which can be accessed by others through that medium. If content is provided from a wide variety of sources then the Internet may can maximise its enormous potential as a source of cultural, political, ethical and linguistic diversity which can increase understanding of cross-cultural issues and perceptions.

As many new and existing entertainment services, including video services, are delivered on-line in a manner which requires a more passive response from

Internet users, it will be increasingly important to ensure that the Internet remains an interactive and participatory experience rather than become a predominantly passive medium.

Illegal Content

Most countries in the world place some restrictions on the type of material which may be possessed and/or disseminated within their borders. The extent and degree to which material in any given country is subject to restrictions reflects its particular political, cultural, religious and legal traditions. These traditions vary immensely around the wcrld. For example, in many countries it is an offence to disseminate certain types of explicitly sexual or extremely violent material. Some countries also make it an offence to publish and/or transmit material which vilifies on the basis of gender, race or sexual orientation. In other countries it is an offence to publish material which criticises the government or may threaten national or racial harmony. In most countries certain dealings concerning child pornography are prohibited.

However, the features of the on-line environment, including the vast amount of content which is available on the Internet, the international source of much of that content and the fact that the Internet is decentralised, make it extremely difficult to prevent material which contravenes the laws of any particular country from being provided or accessed across national boundaries.

The inconsistency between the laws of different countries means that material which may be illegal in one country may be stored and subsequently accessed from countries where the material is legal. It may also be transmitted through a number of other countries, each of which has its own laws regarding the material. Even where there is some consistency across jurisdictions relating to certain material, such as child pornography, the specific provisions of the various laws relating to the topic can differ significantly, making prosecution and international cooperation difficult.

Even determining what is illegal in any particular country can be difficult due to the generality of the various national laws. For example, laws often set out broad categories of restricted material, such as 'obscene' material, and rely on the discretion of courts to give content to the prohibition. This makes it particularly difficult to identify what is prohibited in any given country at any given time.

The ability to communicate anonymously in the on-line environment, which enables users to express themselves in a manner that may not be possible in the off-line world, also renders detection of those providing and accessing material which is prohibited extremely difficult. Anonymous re-mailing services can exacerbate this difficulty as Internet messages can be re-routed and copied in such a way that it is not possible to reliably ascertain their source.

The encryption of content adds a further dimension to the difficulties of dealing with illegal material in the on-line environment.

Material which is Unsuitable for Minors

It is widely accepted around the world that whilst certain kinds of content may be appropriate for adults to access, it may be unsuitable for children. Material which is sexually explicit or violent is often included in the type of content which is considered unsuitable or harmful for minors.

Perceptions about the types of material which are suitable for children and young people vary immensely not only across national boundaries but also across cultures, religions and political systems. In some communities there is a high level of concern regarding sex and nudity, while in others material containing violent matter or drug abuse is considered to be the most offensive. Even within fairly homogeneous cultures there may be a wide range of differing views held about the appropriateness of certain material for minors, particularly where the material relates to sex, nudity, violence, language, and drug use.

In existing media many mechanisms have been adopted to minimise children's access to unsuitable material. These range from age restrictions on material which can be purchased or screened in cinemas to time zone classifications which restrict the type of programs which can be screened on television at times when children are likely to be watching.

However, the availability of material which is considered unsuitable or harmful for minors presents particular challenges in the context of the Internet. The Internet allows material to be accessed at any time in an interactive manner. Most material is not restricted in any way, the main exception being material which requires credit card details or some other form of payment is required. Accordingly, there is growing concern about the ability of minors to access material which is unsuitable for them but at the same time a recognition of the rights of adults to provide and access material which is legal in the off-line world.

In response to this concern a number of technical options, including filter software products and the Platform for Internet Content Selection (PICS) have been developed. These are discussed in more detail below. One of the important challenges in this area will be to ensure that these products are able to accommodate the diverse range of views and cultural perspectives which prevail around the world in relation to the protection of minors.

The Responsibilities of Service Providers in Relation to Content

The international and decentralised nature of the Internet gives rise to a vast range of issues which challenge the mechanism previously used to deal with these matters on a domestic basis. The issues raised in the on-line environment include privacy, intellectual property, defamation, issues of electronic commerce and consumer protection, taxation and on-line gambling, along with illegal content and content which may be harmful to minors, to name a few.

The role and responsibilities which service providers can and should have in relation to these matters is an area in respect of which there has been widespread debate and raises many technical, legal and philosophical issues. Part of the difficulty stems from the complex nature of the service providers role in relation to providing, disseminating and enabling access to content.

In some situations service providers seek to exercise some control over the content that is available through their service whilst in others they may have no knowledge or ability to control the content which is provided or accessed by users or content providers. In such an environment it is extremely difficult to allocate legal responsibility in same the manner that may have been possible in traditional broadcasting and publication models, creating many legal and ethical uncertainties.

Responses To The Challenges Presented By The Internet

As outlined above, the Internet presents immense legal and ethical challenges, particularly in relation to content. It must be accepted that by its very nature the Internet cannot be controlled by any central body and that its dynamic nature means that it is impossible to even assess the amount or nature of Internet content at any given time.

However, many argue that does not mean that nothing can or should be done about content on the Internet. There have been a number of regulatory responses adopted or proposed in several parts of the world which seek to address some of the issues relating to on-line content.

These regulatory responses include:

- the development of codes of practice for service providers with varying degrees of governmental input;
- the application of existing legislation or the introduction of specific legislation penalising dealings with certain on-line content, along with the establishing of e-mail hotlines for the reporting of 'illegal' content;

- technical developments for controlling children's access to Internet content, including filter software and content labelling; and
- the adoption of programs for community education.

A number of international bodies have also begun to consider the issues raised by the growth of the Internet, and the opportunities for international cooperation.

Some of the regulatory responses to the challenges presented by the Internet in each of the countries in the pilot study are now briefly considered.

Industry Codes of Practice

Codes of practice, or codes of conduct as they are sometimes called, are increasingly being used in various industries around the world to provide a regulatory framework which is more flexible than legislation and in respect of which the relevant industry plays an important role. Codes of practice may be developed entirely by industry, or they may be developed following a consultative process between industry and government. In some cases codes of practice operate within class licensing regimes.

Codes of practice, mainly for service providers, are being developed in a number of different countries to try and address some of the issues arising in the on-line environment by setting out goals and best practices for participants in the on-line environment. The codes may deal with a wide range of issues, including but not limited to the rights and responsibilities of relevant parties in regard to providing and accessing content, the minimum age of subscribers, privacy and data protection, fair trading, advertising and promotional material, and the provision of information about the options available to parents to manage children's access to material which may be unsuitable to them.

The pilot study will examine the codes which have emerged or have been proposed in the four countries. Some of the developments which we have identified to date are outlined below.

In Australia a substantially self-regulatory regime for on-line services was recommended by the Australian Broadcasting Authority in its Investigation into the Content of On-Line Services: Report to the Minister for Communications and the Arts, delivered in June 1996 . The report recommended that industry codes of practice should be developed by on-line service providers. The main elements of the proposed regulatory framework are:

- the identification of matters which should be included in codes of practice for service providers, which provide appropriate community safeguards, including complaints handling procedures;
- the registration by the ABA of such codes of practice, developed by service providers after a process of public consultation; and
- the monitoring of the codes of practice, and their effectiveness, by the ABA.

The matters identified for inclusion in the codes include age verification procedures which aim to limit the holding of open on-line accounts to persons over the age of 18 years; the adoption of procedures to deal with illegal material; the provision of information for users and content providers on legislation which may be relevant in an on-line environment; and the provision of information to users regarding filter products or on-line services which are available to those who wish to restrict access to material which may be unsuitable for children. It was also proposed that the codes should encourage content providers to label their content in accordance with PICS compatible labels.

In the United Kingdom the on-line industry has developed a self-regulatory regime which has the support of the Department of Trade and Industry, the Metropolitan Police and the Home Office. The central tenet of the scheme is the Safety-Net initiative which has the support of the Internet Service Providers Association (ISPA), along with the London Internet Exchange (LINX). The scheme involves three key elements; rating content; reporting of content which may be illegal; and the exercise of responsibility by service providers in putting in place appropriate procedures to deal with illegal material once it has been identified.

As part of the scheme ISPA has developed a draft code of practice as a starting point from which a more comprehensive code could be developed. The current draft code requires ISPA members to use their reasonable endeavours to ensure that services and promotional material does not contain content which is in breach of the law; encourages anything which is in any way illegal; contains material which incites violence, sadism, cruelty or racial hatred; or facilitates prostitution. The code also addresses matters of data protection, fair trading, pricing information and complaints procedures.

The United Kingdom Government has stated that service providers who cooperate with the Safety-Net proposals will reduce their risk of prosecution by demonstrating that they have done all that can reasonably be expected to comply with the law .

A somewhat different regulatory scheme has emerged in Singapore. In that country a class licensing scheme for the Internet has been developed . Under the scheme Internet service providers must register with the Singapore Broadcasting Authority (SBA) and comply with the conditions of the class license. All licensed Internet service providers and relevant Internet Content providers are required to comply with the Internet Content Guidelines which have been developed as part of the scheme and satisfy the SBA that they have taken adequate steps to fulfil this requirement . Service providers must also develop Acceptable Use Policies for Internet account holders and comply with any codes of practice as the SBA issues from time to time.

In Malaysia, a major source of regulation to date has been the conditions of service pertaining to the state owned Joint Advanced Research Integrated Networking (JARING) network. These set out the rules applying to Internet services and include the provisions that those using the network shall not use it for any activities not allowed under any law of Malaysia . Until recently the JARING was the only service provider in Malaysia but recently a second operator, Malaysia Telekom Berhad, is reported to have begun trading in Malaysia .

Legislation Relating to On-line Content

As discussed earlier, most countries have some laws which makes it an offence to publish and/or distribute certain material. In some countries it is also an offence to possess certain material, such as child pornography. In some cases existing legislation regarding the publication, distribution and possession of certain types of content has been drafted in a manner which enables it to encompass material transmitted and accessed on-line. However, in other jurisdictions specific legislation to deal with illegal content in the on-line environment has been proposed or introduced.

The pilot study is examining some of the legislation which applies to on-line services in each of the four countries and the types of material which may be prohibited within those jurisdictions. In regard to the type of material which may be illegal in the countries studied the pilot study has, not surprisingly, identified some significant variations in the type of material which would be illegal in each of the countries studied. These variations reflect the range of different political, cultural and religious values which may function in the different jurisdictions.

For example, in Singapore licensees are required to use their best efforts to ensure that their services does not include Internet content which is 'against the public interest, public order, national harmony or which offends against good taste or decency'. The scheme identifies particular Internet content which falls within this category. This includes, inter alia, content "which propagate permissiveness or promiscuity", "tends to bring the Government of Singapore into hatred or contempt, or which excites disaffection against the Government of Singapore." In contrast it seems that at least some content of this nature would not be illegal in the United Kingdom and Australia.

The pilot study will also examine potential liability for illegal content, and consider whether in addition to the content provider, any other party, such as service providers and/or users may incur liability and/or obligations in respect of certain material. In this regard we have found that in Singapore, service providers are required under the class licensing scheme to block access to objectionable sites as directed by the SBA and observe the SBA's content guidelines for subscribing to newsgroups .

In the United Kingdom codes of practice are being utilised to place obligations on service providers to deal with, and where possible, remove illegal content from their servers once it has been identified. In exchange for complying with these procedures service providers may receive some protection from prosecution . In Australia the proposed regulatory regime also envisages that codes of practice for service providers will include appropriate procedures to deal with illegal content if and when it has been brought to a service providers attention. It has been suggested that compliance with codes of practice could be a defence in any prosecution against a service provider.

E-mail Hotlines

One of the recent responses to the issue of illegal content has been the setting up of reporting agencies, often referred to as 'e-mail hotlines'. These agencies enable Internet users who locate content which they believe is illegal to report their finding to a reporting agency which will investigate the content and may take action in relation to the material. To date e-mail hotline services have been identified in Singapore and the United Kingdom.

In the United Kingdom an e-mail hotline has been set up under the Safety-Net Initiative. The Hotline service is operated by Internet Watch and "aims to enhance the enormous potential of the Internet to inform, educate, entertain and conduct business by ... hindering the use of the Internet to transmit material which is illegal in the UK". The first priority of the scheme is child pornography.

Internet Watch operates by encouraging Internet users to report content which they believe to be child pornography. Reports can be made by telephone, facsimile or e-mail and should contain a brief description of the material in question and the location of the site (i.e the world wide web address or the Usenet newsgroup details). Upon receiving a report Internet Watch examines the material and if it considers it illegal will seek to trace its origins. Where the material has been identified as being sourced within the United Kingdom then Internet Watch will request that the relevant service provider contact the person who has placed the material on-line and seek to have the material removed. If material is not removed and/or if it involves child pornography, then Internet Watch will forward details to the Police. Under the scheme the police are to provide feedback to Internet Watch on the outcome of their report. Where the material is sourced from outside of the United Kingdom then Internet Watch will forward to the police the information about the site who will notify the relevant overseas law enforcement agency.

In Singapore, as part of its regulatory regime established in July 1996, the Singapore Broadcasting Authority has also set up a 'hotline' for identifying 'objectionable content'. The SBA has stated that the success of Internet content will depend very much on industry self-regulation and community action and has welcomed public assistance in the identification of material which is considered 'objectionable' under the laws of Singapore. Reports can be made by e-mail, telephone or post .

In Australia the Australian Broadcasting Authority in its Report on the Content of On-Line Services supported in principle the establishment of e-mail hotlines for the reporting of child pornography. The ABA understands that the police bodies and law enforcement bodies are presently examining the viability of establishing such an agency in Australia.

The Protection of Minors in the On-Line Environment

Many argue that parental or teacher supervision is the most effective way of managing children's access to the Internet. However, it is widely recognised that this is not always possible and over the last decade, a range of software products have been developed for use on computers in the home and in schools in response to the perceived need for parents, teachers and supervisors to filter out or block Internet content which they do not consider suitable for minors in their care.

Filter software can be provided to the user by the on-line service provider or purchased independently by the consumer for use at the individual computer level. Some service providers also offer a filtering service which is specifically designed for use by minors. Filtering programs work in three main ways:

- sites are blocked with reference to a list of known newsgroups, world wide web sites, File Transfer Protocol (FTP) and Gopher sites. Censoring decisions may be made centrally by the software producer with sites updated regularly, and/or by users instructing their system to block a particular site(s);

- requests for, or receipt of, information which contains specified keywords or phrases are blocked. The keywords or phrases can be specified by the software manufacturer or by the end users who can manage the blocking of web sites by entering keywords and phrases in accordance with criteria they consider appropriate; and
- all sites are blocked except those which are specified by the supervisor ('blanket blocking'). These programs usually provide an original unblocked list of known educational sites, and the supervisor is able to unblock new sites through a password secured interface.

Some products enable parents to combine some of these functions, while others offer additional features such as auditing of all on-line activity, including listing sites accessed, restricting the amount of time spent on-line and limiting access to some services such as bulletin boards.

Whilst the first generation of filter products offer parents some tools to control their children's access to unsuitable material, some users have found that they have a number of limitations. For example, products which are based on recognition of keywords and phrases are not able to filter explicit graphic images or deal with encrypted data or transposed text. Conversely, sites of value to the user may also be blocked if they contain specified keywords or phrases. For example, press reports stated that at one time access to the White House web site was blocked by a filter responding to the word 'couple'.

Where software producers are responsible for the blocking of material they may restrict content which is considered acceptable to the parent/supervisor. Where filter software operates by means of 'blanket' blocking, access to a considerable amount of potentially valuable material would be denied and parents and teachers would in many cases have to allocate considerable resources to enable access to appropriate material.

However, there have been some recent international developments with content and selection software which have provided additional options for parents. This technology is called the Platform for Internet Content Selection (PICS). PICS was developed by the World Wide Web Consortium (W3C). W3C is a non-governmental cross-industry group which has offices in USA, France and Japan and comprises representatives of the computer, communications and content industries, as well as trade associations and public interest groups.

PICS works by establishing a series of file formats that allows independent rating services to label Internet content in a form that can be recognised by PICS enabled software. The PICS labelling conventions do not dictate the use of any particular labelling scheme or determine who should pay attention to which labels. The PICS technology allows any organisation or individual to develop a labelling system which reflects their tastes and standards and, if they wish, enable others to also use these labels. PICS compatible software can be set to block out all unrated content, or to only block content which has been rated in a certain manner.

There are a number of scenarios in which PICS labels can be used. For example, labels may be developed to indicate whether Internet content contains sexual or violent material, enabling parents to select or block the material accordingly. A teacher might label a set of materials which are relevant to an astronomy lesson and block student access to everything else during that class.

Those concerned about Nazi propaganda and other hate-speech available on-line, could label material that is historically inaccurate or that promotes hate, and businesses may wish to use labels to block their employees from visiting recreational sites during hours of office hours .

Labelling can be applied directly by content providers at the time or after a site is posted on the Internet or it can be applied by a third party in accordance with an established labelling system.

The creators of PICS envisaged that it could be used to support a large number of different labelling schemes which may have a multitude of different purposes. A number of organisations have already begun to establish labelling schemes which can interact with the PICS standards, most of which have been developed in North America and aim to assist parents in managing their children's access to Internet content. Examples are the Recreational Software Advisory Council labelling scheme for the Internet (RSACi), SafeSurf, Cyber Patrol and Net Shepherd.

One of the PICS compatible labelling schemes which has gained increasing prominence is the descriptive labelling scheme developed by the Recreational Software Advisory Council (RSAC) and is discussed below by way of example.

The RSACi labelling system addresses four matters. These are the level of violence, sex, nudity, and language, including hate language, which a site contains. Internet content can be given a rating between 0 and 4 on each of these topics. The label aims to provide a description of the content in an Internet site rather than make a judgement about the appropriateness of content for any given audience or purpose. In some ways the descriptive RSAC labels can be seen as analogous to the labels applied to foodstuffs which merely provide information about ingredients of a product, rather than vouch for its suitability for consumption.

One of the uses of a descriptive labelling schemes is that it enables parents to set their own standards about the material which they or their children access. For example, parents who are concerned about sexual content are able to set their PICS compatible software to block out material which has been given a high rating for sexual content. Other parents may be more concerned about language and/or violence and so can also can set their software to block out highly rated material of this nature. If the material has been rated then parents can use the labels to control Internet content, regardless of where they or the content is located.

Importantly, those who are not concerned to block their own access to Internet materials need not activate those tools.

A proliferation of PICS compatible labelling schemes, perhaps being developed by a range of industry, community and governmental bodies around the world could serve many functions, including giving consumers a range of choices in relation to the values and perspectives which underpin the various labelling schemes and the purposes for which they can be used. This has the ability to reflect a diversity of different cultures and values and provide individuals with real choices about the filtering software and nature of Internet content which they access.

However, for labels to be a truly effective tool for parents and supervisors many argue that a critical mass of content needs to be labelled. This raises the issue of whether it would be advantageous to develop a small number of international labelling schemes which can be widely recognised by content providers and users around the globe.

The pilot study will examine the steps taken, if any, in each of the four countries to address the issue of children's access to unsuitable material on the Internet. This will include any programs adopted or recommendations made in relation to filtering systems and PICS compatible labelling schemes.

To date we have found that the Safety-Net initiative developed in the United Kingdom originally supported the use of the RSACi labeling scheme and proposed that service providers require their users to rate their web sites using RSACi labels.

However, the ABA understands that there have been some recent developments in this regard and that Internet Watch Foundation has undertaken to work with the on-line industry in that country to develop a PICS compatible labeling scheme which meets the specific requirements of users in the United Kingdom.

In Australia labelling Internet content was given detailed consideration in the ABA's Report into the Content of On-Line Services. While recognising that labelling schemes might have many uses, the protection of children from unsuitable material was seen as one of the primary uses. The Report recommended that an On-Line Labelling Task Force be established to encourage development of an Australian labelling scheme for on-line content which was compatible with PICS or any superior standards which might be developed.

The ABA is also conscious of the need to ensure that an Australian Labelling scheme is, as far as possible, consistent with international ratings developments. This is to ensure that Australian content providers and users of the labelling schemes are not disadvantaged in terms of both having Australian content accessed by users around the world, or accessing a wide variety of material when using utilising the labels.

Under the Singaporean regulatory regime for on-line services, localized service providers and parents are encouraged to use filter software products such as Net Nanny, SurfWatch, Cyber Patrol and Net Shepherd . The ABA notes that some of these filter products are compatible with the PICS standards.

As an additional measure to protect young Internet users the SBA also requires schools, libraries and Internet service providers which provide access to children to institute tighter levels of controls. The SBA has announced that it is presently working with the Minister of Education and National Library Board to identify options for implementing an acceptable level of control .

Programs for Community Educational

The potential benefits of the on-line environment for enhancing the way we communicate, educate, inform and entertain ourselves has been widely recognised. However, it is also recognised that community understanding of the nature of on-line services, including the opportunities which they present and the options available for managing children's access to those services will be critical if the Internet is to be used in the most productive manner.

Many countries have adopted or proposed strategies for enhance community understanding of the Internet and the opportunities which it offers. A priority for many of these programs is parental education, as many parents feel that they do not have as much experience in relation to on-line services as their children and therefore are unable to effectively utilise some of the technical options available to them for limiting children's access to unsuitable Internet content.

A number of programs have also been proposed or introduced to enhance the knowledge and technical ability of teachers who will play an important role in ensuring that children are able to maximise the benefits of on-line services.

The pilot study is examining proposals in the four countries to enhance community understanding of on-line services, including proposals for the educational sector. To date we have identified a number of proposals and programs.

In Australia the importance of community education in terms of promoting the most beneficial use of the Internet and ensuring that users, particularly parents, were aware of the options available for managing children's access was recognised in the ABA's Report on its Investigation into On-line Services.

The report recommended, inter alia, that a community education strategy be developed to provide information about on-line services and that the strategy target parents and guardians. It was proposed that information might be distributed via school and parent networks, at the point of sale for computer hardware and software, as well as on relevant web sites.

The report also recommended that research be undertaken by the ABA and other relevant bodies to assist in determining the requirements of parents and guardians in relation to managing children's access to Internet content.

There have also been a number of initiatives developed in the school environment. These include the Education Network Australia (EdNA) project which obtained in principle agreement form all Australian, State and Territory Governments at a meeting of the Ministerial Council on Education, Employment, Training and Youth Affairs in May 1995. The project aims to provide Australia wide access to educational products and services relevant to Australian educators .

Another project which has been developed is oz-TeacherNet.This is a service which has been developed to meet the needs of teachers to make greater use of the resources, professional development and curriculum opportunities which the Internet offers.

In terms of student usage, a number of different approaches have been adopted by schools to manage access to unsuitable material, including the development of acceptable use policies, student contracts, and restricting access to particular sites or Internet functions such as newsgroups at the school or service provider level.

In Malaysia, as part of the drive to ensure the success of the Multimedia Super Corridor (MSC), a number of major initiatives are being undertaken. One of these is the connection of all schools within the MSC to the Internet by 1998. In a speech for the opening of Multimedia Asia on 1 August 1996, the Prime Minister of Malaysia, Yab Dato Seri Dr Mahathir Bin Mohamad announced that the Malaysian Government is working to increase the role of multimedia in education:

> Teachers will need to change their role in the electronic classroom from being information providers to counsellors in order to help the students know how to select information sources, to make judgements about what they are downloading ... The measure of our success in 2020 will be the number and quality of our people who can add value to information. To that end, we will be creating a Multimedia University and technology schools within the MSC.

In Singapore the SBA has expressed an intention to complement its regulatory regime with public education initiatives which alert parents to the ways in which they may protect their children from 'objectionable material and cyberspace abuses'. As part of its strategy the SBA has also set up a web site called 'Tips for Parents' page.

In the UK there have been a number of initiatives undertaken by various organisations which seek, amongst other things, to enhance community understanding of the Internet and provide some guidance for parents on how they might manage their children's use of the Internet. NCH Action for Children, Britain's largest child care charity, provides an example of a non-government organisation (NGO) on-line initiative aimed at educating parents about the Internet . The organisation's web site includes a 'Parent's Guide to the Internet' and advice on getting the best from the Internet. It also attempts to explain some commonly used Internet jargon, as well as provides some useful contacts.

These contacts include the NETCOM parent's advice line, a 24 hour telephone advice line, and the parents information network. The network is a national information technology organisation offering help to parents who want to use computers with their children. The 'Useful Contacts' page also includes hyperlinks to the PICS and RSACi web sites.

In July 1996 the House of Lords Select Committee on Science and Technology published a report titled Information Society: Agenda for Action in the UK on 23 July 1996. The report contained 40 recommendations for action to promote the development of the Information Society. A number dealt with information technology in schools and the Government has responded to the Report with a number of strategies to improve teacher competence in this area and increase the number of schools connected to the Internet.

Some International Responses

There has been an increasingly amount of discussion regarding the importance of international cooperation in maximising the opportunities and meeting some of the challenges presented by the Internet. Two international bodies who have recently focussed on these issues are the European Commission (EC) and Organisation for Economic Cooperation and Development (OECD). It is interesting to note that the areas which have been identified for action are consistent with some of the regulatory responses taken in the countries in the pilot study.

The European Commission (EC), in its Green Paper on the Protection of Minors and Human Dignity in Audiovisual and Information Services, considered that the main tasks which the on-line industry should address are:

- drawing up a code of conduct and concrete measures within a framework defined by cooperation between national government departments;
- identifying areas where there may be a need for common standards on the labelling of material; and
- promoting the PICS standard or equivalent systems with a view to reaching, as quickly as possible, a critical mass of labelled material, navigation systems and/or parental control devices which are mutually compatible.

The Report of the European Commission's Working Party on Illegal and Harmful Content on the Internet has also proposed, inter alia, that a self-regulatory scheme be developed for the on-line environment comprising:

- a code of conduct for Internet service providers, including access providers, host service providers and anonymous re-mailers; ?a hot-line for complaints from the public, with appropriate safeguards against misuse; and
- an independent self-regulatory body, including representatives of industry and users, to advise on whether or not a breach of the code of conduct has occurred (without prejudice to the due process of law).

The Organisation for Economic and Cultural Development (OECD) has recently been asked to consider two proposals concerning the regulation of the Internet. The first of these is a proposal of the French Government for a general agreement on international cooperation for regulation of the Internet with a view to enhancing the economic and cultural potential of the Internet and to combat illegal activities. The proposal points to three priority areas for cooperation:

- the definition of a typology of players and the methodological rules to be applied;
- a list of guidelines aimed at guaranteeing the respect of basic ethical rules and improving consumer protection; and
- principles for judicial and police cooperation.

It is also proposed that signatories to the agreement will promote the establishment by economic players of a voluntary code of conduct. The codes are to safeguard various principles, including the principle of respect for human dignity and of public order (in particular through use of filtering software), the principle of protection of privacy, and the principle of consumer protection.

The Belgian government has also recently put forward a proposal to the OECD for a convention aimed at prohibiting the transmission on the Internet of content that encourages the exploitation of and sexual violence to children. The ABA understands that this matter is presently being considered by the Committee for Information, Computer and Communications Policy (ICCP).

The unique features of the Internet give rise to an environment which provides enormous opportunities for enhanced communication and civic participation, education and entertainment for individuals and organisations around the world. The Internet has the potential to reflect a diverse range of cultural, political, religious and linguistic perspectives and enhance our understanding of across different cultures.

But along with these immense opportunities, the Internet also presents a number of particular challenges. The Pilot Study being carried out by the ABA for

UNESCO will examine some of the legal, cultural and ethical issues which have emerged from the growth of the Internet. The study also aims to provide a valuable body of comparative data on the regulatory frameworks developed or proposed in four countries in response to these challenges. When completed the pilot study will be provided on-line so that it can be accessed by users around the world.

This comparative 'stocktake' of developments in a range of countries may provide a useful reference point for considering international trends. It might also assist in the process of identifying potential areas of international cooperation and enable the Internet to maximise the benefits and opportunities which it can offer the individuals and communities around the world.

8

Privacy on Internet

The linguistic meanings of the term privacy according to Webster's Dictionary are: "1. (a) the quality or state of being apart from company or observation: seclusion (b) freedom from unauthorized intrusion. 2 archaic: a place for seclusion. 3: secrecy".

In the classical legal terminology according to Black's Law Dictionary, the right of privacy is: "The right to be let alone; the right of a person to be free from unwarranted publicity; and right to live without unwarranted interference by the public in matters with which the public is not necessarily concerned".

The term 'right of privacy' is a generic term encompassing various rights recognized to be inherent in the concept of ordered liberty, and such right prevents governmental interference in intimate personal relationships or activities, freedoms of individual to make fundamental choices involving himself, his family, and his relationship with others. The right of an individual (or corporation) to withhold himself and his property from public scrutiny, if he so chooses. It is said to exist only so far as its assertion is consistent with law or public policy, and in a proper case equity will interfere, if there is no remedy at law, to prevent an injury threatened by the invasion of, or infringement upon, this right from motives of curiosity, gain of malice". According to the same source the invasion of privacy encompasses acts such as "the unwarranted appropriation or exploitation of one's personality, publicizing one's private affairs with which the public has no legitimate concern, or wrongful intrusion into one's private activities, in such a manner to cause mental suffering, shame or humiliation to person of ordinary sensibilities. The violation of the right which one has to be left alone and unnoticed if he so chooses. Such invasion by an individual or the government may constitute an actionable tort.The invasion of privacy is perpetrated by acts such as eavesdropping or using pen register".

According to modern legal concepts the following aspects of an individual's right of privacy in the context of rights in electronic information as stated by Thomas J. Smedingoff 6 are: "Privacy of a Person's persona: Certain privacy rights attached to a person's persona- that is, a person's name, identity, photograph, voice and so forth. Any misuse of that persona can constitute an invasion of that right of privacy. Privacy of Data About a Person: Privacy rights can also attach to information about a person that is collected and used by others. This might include, for example, information about a person's spending habits, medical history, religious or political affiliations, tax records, employment records, insurance records, criminal records, and the like. Misuse of this information by collecting organizations or their customers has often been a source of controversy. Privacy of a

Person's Communications: There is also, in certain situations, a right of privacy with respect to online communications sent to or from an individual. Thus, in certain circumstances, monitoring or disclosing the contents of an electronic communication by anyone other than the sender or the intended recipient can constitute an invasion of privacy. Anonymity: Finally, there is the ultimate form of privacy "anonymity." Anonymity often plays an important role in online electronic communication. The extent to which anonymity is a right, and ought to be respected, is also the subject of much controversy".

According to modern jurisprudence the privacy of a person's online communications may be violated by the unlawful interception of electronic communications, the unlawful accessing of stored electronic information and communications and the unlawful divulgence of the anonymity of a person.

On the De Jure side, the right of privacy is regulated both internationally and nationally by many legal tools such as: International treaties and conventions, directives, national constitutions, national acts, legislations, regulations, etc. describing rights and prescribing penalties on the offenders (if caught). Contractual undertakings could be a protective element between contracting parties. Also, self-regulation measures are available to control the behaviour of the members of groups with special interests but with a lesser effect. The protection of privacy on the networks is provided on the De Facto side by technological devices and procedures in the realm of communication security comprising: physical security, encryption, TX security, emission security 8. Information and communication security is the first and most effective line of defense to protect privacy on the networks to safeguard communications from the (six Es: error, embezzlement, extortion, enmity, espionage and ego). This is to be followed by the legal deterrent and ethics consecutively by order of effectiveness.

The Invasion of Privacy on the Networks

Before embarking on this short trip through the legal framework of the ways and means for the protection of the Right of Privacy on the networks, we should start by viewing some socio-economic factors, which are the roots of this issue, culminating in a behavioural problem. The impacts of Globalization, Relativism, the New World Order, Materialism, Egocentricism, Hyper Consumerism, invasive technologies (we should not forget the positive effects of scientific and technological achievements), the uncontrollable flood of information, the advent of genetic manipulation and perhaps genetic control, the corrosion of the notion of the sacred in modern post-industrial societies and many other factors have disturbed the ladder of values in each and every society. The insatiable greed for more instant pleasure (which is not in itself a sin) has added a spinning (or perhaps a cataclysmic) potential to the tempo of change. Due to this uncontrollable hyper acceleration in all the venues of life including cyber crime, some would state that a rational utilitarian scale of values could govern human behaviour. But let us remember that Auguste Comte (Catechisme Positive) did not solve the problem, ideologies also failed due to the gap between theory and practice. The human being cannot be ethically perfect; philosophers do not rule the world and the pure rational man does not exist. The paradox between stability and change remains and perhaps the tools of global behavioural control shall prevail in the future eliminating in their way what is known as free will (if any?).

We return to the privacy issue by examining some practices which are sometimes illegal and sometimes legal and which have an impact on the privacy on the networks:

As mentioned in Sautter's report "To prevent the loss of hundreds of thousands of dollars in wasted man-hours and bandwidth more and more employers are using special software to monitor their employees' Web browsing and e-mail traffic".

Marketers can spy on you by using cookies. A cookie is a unique text file that is placed on your hard drive the first time you access certain websites. It is like a personal serial number used to identify your computer on your next visit to the site but the cookie also enables the marketers to gather information about your browsing preferences. According to the Washington based privacy research group EPIC, 86 out of 100 tested online companies work with cookies. The gathered information about the customers could be sold to other persons or entities".

Hackers can spy on you by using Trojan horses coming in the guise of backdoor computer programs which once infiltrating into your computer allows hackers to access it and take control. Hackers can even spy on your E-mail as it passes through the several web servers. At any of these relay points your message is vulnerable to snooping. Skillful hackers can also hijack a router and then read or mess around with the text messages stored in it. Sniffer programs may scan traffic for specified terms, cyber snoops can capture Internet account login IDS & passwords and use them to surf the web at owner's expense and web based E-mail services are particularly open to intruders".

Some sovereign states run electronic surveillance systems around the world and scan the web for signs of criminal activity, monitoring E-mail communications eavesdropping on chat room conversations and generally tracking the traffic on the net. Echelon, a massive cold war-era surveillance network run by the intelligence services of the U.S., U.K., Canada New Zealand and Australia, is the world's most extensive spy system for nonmilitary targets and the one most likely to be watching as you roam the Web. Some 90% of Net traffic is said to be scanned by Echelon. Several countries also run their own national Web surveillance systems. According to Duncan Campbell "the Echelon system can access and process all of the world's satellite communications automatically". A large part of Echelon is devoted to the INTELSAT network of Geo stationary communications satellites. Cable tapping is harder, however, as with cryptography itself Echelon is fighting a loosing battle. As more and more phones become low power digital devices, the range over which they can be monitored and the effort needed to decode them increases, a brand new wireless technology called pulse wireless - already used by the security services - promises to make many transmission virtually undetectable". By autumn of this year, the Echelon interception system will be subject to a legal battle that threatens to blow the lid on this covert surveillance network Echelon when the issue reaches the courts. David Nataf of the Jean Pierre Millet law firm in Paris is leading the assault on America's National Security Agency (NSA). The plaintiffs, several French corporations and individuals who cannot be identified, allege that the

(NSA) has spied on them illegally". He says his team has enough evidence against the (NSA) to pursue damages for lost business and for illegal covert activity. At the center of the allegations is evidence implicating the (NSA's) involvement in spying on European nations' commercial dealings. Nataf's team will try to convince the American courts that stolen information was passed onto US companies, giving them an unfair advantage over their French competitors. In March 2000, a former CIA director, James Woolsey, confirmed that the US monitors European communications to keep an eye on any economic bribery activities. "We have spied on that (bribery) in the past," said Woolsey responding to the (Interception Capabilities 2000) report presented to the parliament's Citizens Rights Committee. "I hope that the United States government continues to spy on bribery". The controversial impact of Echelon was also apparent on a broader platform, in July 2000 the European Parliament voted to set up a Temporary Committee of inquiry on the Echelon interception system.

"Governments may not be the only ones spying on citizens' secrets." It is suggested that multinational companies may have taken their cue from Echelon and are carrying out their own surveillance work. Some have suggested they may even cooperate with secret government snooping. Industrial espionage is not a new phenomenon, but as information becomes ever more vital to companies and integral to their practices it is easy to see that the incentives are greater than ever. A Scientific and Technical Options Assessment (STOA) report called Development of Surveillance Technology and Risk of Abuse of Economic Information presented to the European Union December 1999 concludes that: "Although it is very difficult to quantify the losses caused by industrial espionage, the losses incurred by European firms can reasonably be put at several billion Euros per year".

These are some of the issues affecting the Right of Privacy on the networks. The matrix of interceptors includes individuals, corporations, multinational companies and even sovereign states. Efforts are evolving to inquire into these interception activities and even to condone their acts pursuant to the right of privacy on the networks and global communication.

Fact or fiction. As with any issue involving communities at large, a multitude of interception techniques have been described and elaborated on. Some even sound extremely credible and others are generally discarded as unimaginable at the current state of technology. Duncan Campbell's study (Interception Capabilities 2000) attempts to portray the current technological capabilities available. A summary of the key findings concerning the state of the art in (Comint) are: "Comprehensive systems exist to access, intercept, and process every important modern form of communications, with few exceptions; Contrary to reports in the press, effective (word spotting) search systems that have the capability to automatically select telephone calls of intelligence interest are not yet available, despite 30 years of research. However, speaker recognition systems - in effect, (voiceprints) - have been developed and are deployed to recognize the speech of targeted individuals making international telephone calls; Recent diplomatic initiatives by the United States government seeking European agreement to the (key escrow) system of cryptography masked intelligence collection requirements have formed part of a long-term program which has undermined and continues to undermine the communications privacy of non-US nationals, including European governments, companies and citizens; there is wide-ranging evidence indicating that major governments are routinely utilizing communications intelligence to provide commercial advantage to companies and trade".

The Legal Protection of the Right of Privacy On the Networks in the Modern World

The law has a functional role by deterring any potential perpetrator from committing a criminal act and it also has a curative effect in devolving compensations for damages if an illicit act is committed. The legal texts covering this area are various as we have previously mentioned and they constitute two faces of one coin. One face is information protection laws and the other is telecommunications protection laws. Their symbiotic effect produces the legal deterrent and protection.

To be criminalized and penalized by the law, the acts of violation of the right of privacy should constitute crimes in conformity with the old Latin rule (Nullum Crimen, Nulla Poena Sine Lege). We should bear in mind that criminal law texts are interpreted very strictly (stricto sensu). In the modern world, we first find on the international level the international agreements and conventions such as: I-The Universal Declaration of Human Rights in which Article 12 states that: "No one shall be subjected to arbitrary interference with his privacy,ÿor correspondence,ÿEveryone has the right to the protection of the law against such interference". A key word in this Article is (arbitrary). Lawful interference is not excluded.

II- The International Covenant on Civil and Political Rights. This UN Covenant builds on the Universal Declaration and is legally binding. By Art. 2.1, the Contracting Parties are obliged to respect and ensure all of the rights recognized by the Covenant, and by Art. 2.2 they are required to take steps to meet their obligations within their own legal systems. Art. 4 allows Contracting Parties to derogate from some of the specific Articles (i.e. Rights) in a Public Emergency. Article 17 states that: "No one shall be subjected to arbitrary or unlawful interference with his privacy" and that: "Everyone has a right to the protection of the law against such interference". This appears to address only natural, not legal persons and reinforces the idea that lawful interference is permitted".

The second layer of legal sources comprises the national legislations either enacted by parliament in the form of legislations and acts or in some countries by means of presidential decrees and in said context, we state the situation of the legislation in some developed countries. In the U.S.A., privacy on the networks is protected by "the Federal Electronic Communications Act (ECPA), which protects all forms of electronic communications - telephone voice communications as well as computer digital communication. ECPA applies to the government as well as private persons and entities. It prohibits any person from intentionally, intercepting an electronic communication, or from disclosing the contents of any intercepted electronic communication unlawfully. It applies not only to hackers but also to those who own and operate such systems such as an internet access provider, a private network operator, the sys-op of a computer bulletin board and the like. ECPA also prohibits any person or entity who provides an electronic communication service to the public from divulging the contents of any communication. The anonymity of communications emanates according to the U.S. Supreme Court from the right to speak anonymously and is protected by the first amendment to the US constitution 6. ECPA in the USA sets in place a procedure to authorize lawful interception. Network operators and service providers are required by CALEA (the Communication Assistance for Law Enforcement Act) to have the necessary technical facility and to render assistance to law enforcement agencies.

The Foreign Intelligence Surveillance Act of 1978 (FISA) authorized electronic surveillance of foreign powers and agents of foreign powers is regulated to protect the US national security. To target communications need not relate to any crime, FISA surveillance action are implemented operationally by FBI. Said surveillance is classified. In addition to said legal vehicles the Privacy Act of 1974 imposes limits on the collection and use of personal information by federal government agencies. The Privacy Protection Act of 1980 establishes safeguards relating to materials held by a person reasonably believed to have a purpose to publish a newspaper, book, broadcast, or similar public communication.

The Fair Credit Reporting Act of 1970 regulates information maintained by creditors. The Right to Financial Privacy Act restricts government access to the financial report of any financial institutional customer. The Telephone Consumer Protection Act of 1991 protects the consumer from advertising via e-mail.

In addition to a plethora of state laws and regulations.

However, the situation in the European Union is thoroughly exposed as can be seen in the comprehensive study prepared by Dr. Chris Elliot for the scientific and technological option assessment program of the European Parliament. According to the executive summary of said precious study "the EU countries are committed by international treaties, EU decisions and directives and each national country by its national laws. Most countries have legal recognition of the right of privacy of personal data and many require telecommunications network operators to protect the privacy of their users.

All EU countries permit the use of encryption for data transmitted via public telecommunications networks (except France where this will shortly be permitted). Electronic commerce requires secure and trusted communications and may not be able to benefit from privacy law designed only to protect natural persons. The legal regimes reflect a balance between three interests: privacy; law enforcement; electronic commerce. Legal processes are emerging to satisfy the second and third interests by granting more power to governments to authorize interception (under legal controls) and allowing strong encryption with secret keys. There do not appear to be adequate legal processes to protect privacy against unlawful interception, either by foreign governments or by non-governmental bodies. A course of action open to the EU is to require telecommunications operators to take greater precautions to protect their users against unlawful interception. This would appear to be possible without compromising law enforcement or electronic commerce"

The right of privacy on the networks in a developing country (Egypt as a case study)

The right of privacy is governed in Egypt as in several other countries by consecutive layers of legal texts both on the supranational and the national levels. On the international level, Article 12 of The Universal Declaration Of Human Rights together with The International Covenants On The Civil And Political Rights are enforced according to Article 151 Para 1 of the Egyptian Constitution which stipulates the following: "The President of the republic shall conclude treaties and communicate them to the People's Assembly, accompanied with a suitable clarification. They shall have the force of law after their conclusion, ratification, and publication according to the established procedure".

On the constitutional level, article 45 of the Egyptian Constitution stipulates the following: "The law shall protect the inviolability of the private life of citizens. Correspondence, wires, telephone calls and other means of communication shall have their own sanctity and secrecy and may not be confiscated, divulged or monitored, except by a causal judicial warrant and for a definite period according to the provisions of the law". And in the same context Article 57 of the Constitution stipulates: "Any assault on individual freedom or on the inviolability of private life of citizens and any other public rights and liberties guaranteed by the Constitution and the law shall be considered a crime, whose criminal and civil lawsuit is not liable to prescription. The State shall grant a fair compensation to the victim of such an assault". We would like to state also that before the prevailing Constitution of 1971 the previous Constitutions including the Constitution of 1923 safeguarded the right of privacy by stipulating in Article 11 "It is prohibited to divulge the secrets contained in letters, telegrams, phone communication except in the cases provided for in the law".

On the legislative level, secrecy and privacy are maintained in several legislations such as Tax Laws, Banking Secrecy Law, The Laws pertaining to Correspondence and mail the laws pertaining to the Civil Status, the laws governing Statistics and Census, the Code of Criminal Procedures, the Penal Code and the Civil Code.

From the analysis of the texts of the constitution and the several legislations previously mentioned, we can conclude the following:

a) The right of privacy pertaining to personal data and information is protected both by constitutional texts and by legislative texts.

b) Eavesdropping, hacking, and unlawful surveillance by using phone lines as a medium of communication are penalized by the texts of the penal code. In the opinion of the majority of the Egyptian jurisprudence.

c) In my opinion, privacy on the networks is in general protected by the texts of the prevailing laws.

d) To ensure maximum protection, amendments should be made to the text of Article 309 of the Egyptian Penal Code. To penalize eavesdropping, unlawful intrusion, or penetration or unlawful surveillance of telecommunications since the prevailing law protects phone conversations and the penal law is interpreted in the strict sense (stricto sensu)

e) A new law governing telecommunications is on its way to being discussed by the new parliament to be elected, this law organizes telecommunication. In said draft of law an article governing the secrecy of telecommunication is appearing. We shall see the final product after its enactment by the competent constitutional authorities.

f) Contractual undertakings to safeguard privacy may be added to any contracts.

Further elaboration leads me to display that the current Egyptian Civil Law distinctly provides for the right to demand for compensation sustained independently from the right of the state to impose penalties. Egyptian Civil Law stipulates in Article 50 the following:

"A person whose rights inherent in his personality have been unlawfully infringed, shall have the right to demand the cessation of the infringement and compensation for any damage sustained thereby". And it stipulates in Article 163 the following: "Every fault which causes injury to another, imposes an obligation to make reparation upon the person by whom it is committed".

Accordingly, the sanctity of the right of privacy is protected by the civil law. If the right of privacy has been unlawfully infringed, the victim of said infringement shall have the right to demand before a court of law the cessation of infringement and compensation for any damage sustained thereby.

The right to receive the compensation for damages according to the civil law is an independent right from the right of the state to impose corporal or financial penalties on the perpetrator of a crime committed in violation to the Right of Privacy and as mentioned previously. The perpetrator is penalized if proven guilty by imprisonment and/or fine.

The Impact of the Conflict of Laws And the Conflict of Jurisdictions on Law Enforcement

Our modern world is composed of independent sovereign states. Each sovereign state has its own constitution, laws, and competent courts. As a result of said situation, each law in each sovereign state determines the material acts that constitute a crime. As state laws differ in general from country to country, we are sometimes faced with the quandary of conflicting laws. Some examples can be as follows:

Networks intrusion could be considered as a criminal act in a state and not considered as such in another state.

A sovereign state may have a law penalizing the hacking and interception of messages on the networks and another state may not have in its legislations any text penalizing said act.

In the same context, a sovereign state may penalize the breaking of its laws by an individual who commits a criminal act on the networks from the territory of a country in which the act is not penalized and prosecute said person and try him in absentia and from said trial a verdict of guilt and a sentence of imprisonment could emanate, how could said state execute the sentence on the perpetrator who is the citizen of another sovereign state whose laws do not penalize said act?

An individual may act innocently on the networks with a party in another sovereign state without real knowledge of the laws of the country with whom he is accessing through the networks and most probably said country would have a criminal text penalizing his behaviour and most probably another legal text stating that (ignorance of the law is no defense). Furthermore, some procedural laws in several sovereign states would give to the public prosecution the right to prosecute specific crimes such as attempts to disrupt the national security of a state even if the act is perpetrated outside of the borders of said sovereign country. Accordingly, the conflict of laws is a crucial topic pertaining to the governance of the legal conduct on the networks.

The conflict of jurisdictions is another issue triggered by the fact that different Courts in different countries may be considered by each and every sovereign state as the competent courts to see into a case. The law of one country may indicate that a criminal court is competent to try an eavesdropping crime on the networks perpetrated by a citizen of a foreign country against an individual or an entity in the first country. On the other hand, the foreign country and according to its procedural laws may consider its courts competent since its citizen committed the crime on the soil of said country. A third country may consider its courts competent to view the same case before a state security court and not before a traditional criminal court since the act is considered according to said third country laws a state security crime (i.e. espionage). In one federal state, you may find conflict of laws and conflict of jurisdictions between state laws and federal laws, state courts and federal courts.

International treaties and conventions are the tools used in international law to homogenize the legal principles in the different sovereign states and to harmonize the stipulations of the different national laws & to solve the conflicts. Due to the international aspect of most of the crimes perpetrated via the Internet or the other networks, the reasonable and ideal solution according to some lawyers would be the governance of the international networks by an international treaty containing positive clauses governing the behaviour of the individuals and entities on the networks and penalizing any infringement of the clauses of said treaty through international prosecution, courts and law enforcement agencies. Said idealistic approach should give rise to an international judiciary able and capable to issue orders and verdicts enforceable against the perpetrators of any criminal act on the net in the various jurisdictions. Said solution is a farfetched solution.

A compromise could be reached by having an international treaty stating minimum requirements in the different national laws to safeguard the right of privacy and other rights on the net. In many countries including Egypt treaties and conventions when signed, approved, promulgated, and enacted by the parliament have the force of the national laws. Also, the European model in this context is one of the successful models (through the regional conventions, European Directives etc.) the model of the United States of America pertaining to the relation between the different states of the union and the supremacy of the federal laws. The elaboration by jurists and professionals of a model law to be used as an example by sovereign states to legislate internal laws, is also another solution.

However, enforcement of the Law is a crucial issue facing several problems. In an attempt to display the current inherent difficulties faced in enforcement of the law:

- The anonymity of the perpetrator;
- The quasi immateriality of the criminal act that should be proven before a court of law according to procedural laws which are not always modeled to

tackle cyber crime issues and especially the immateriality of the conduct on the networks and the immateriality of the evidence;

- The technical incapability of most police forces to track and apprehend the perpetrator on line;
- The geographical and territorial barriers (the world is communication wise a global village but law enforcement wise it is composed of geographically separated continents countries); and
- The preoccupation of the police force with other types of conventional crimes which are called natural crimes or with other life threatening crimes or national security issues and not with cyber crimes against natural personsÿ and many more aspects.

This enumeration is not a complete list but a count of the more relevant aspects that should be taken into consideration regarding enforcement of the law against perpetrators.

Remarks and Suggestions

Remarks

— The struggle between the individuals or the entities seeking the protection of their right of privacy and the intruders shall remain.

— The technological race between privacy protection techniques and surveillance techniques shall continue at least for the foreseen future.

— Technical protection remains the most effective line of defense for the privacy on the networks.

— The different modes and degrees of legal protection in different countries together with the international aspect of the acts, the conflict of laws and the conflict of jurisdictions remain a setback for the criminalization and penalization of acts constituting violations of privacy on the network.

— The anonymity of the perpetrator remains an obstacle and the quasi immateriality of the cyber crime is a problem pertaining to the acceptable evidence to be produced before a court of law.

— The preoccupation of law enforcement agencies with other crimes which are in their opinion more important than the crimes against the right of privacy is another negative aspect in this context.

— The unavailability of funds to provide for the technical backing of the law enforcement agencies in their war against intruders is a detrimental factor.

— The technical aspect of cyber crimes in itself poses a problem to the law enforcement agencies due to the technical sophistication of the acts and the inaptitude of most legal practitioners to add the required legal qualification to said acts of violation of the right of privacy to qualify them as illicit acts.

— The attitude of some sovereign states towards the issue of the Right of Privacy on the networks and its effect on national security drives some sovereign states to have a reserved position pertaining to the right of privacy on the networks fearing its negative impact in matters of national security (comprising political security, economic security and social security). The issue of national security is a relative matter differing from one state to the other. The declared position of a country may be contradictory to its undeclared position.

— Hyper materialism and conventional ethics are incompatible.

Suggestions

— A multi disciplinary approach for the protection of the right of privacy is the available approach up till now mixing the propagation of applicable and practical ethical values for the conduct on the networks together with an applicable legal deterrent penalizing the perpetrators for any violation of the right of privacy, this is in addition to the first line of defense which is the use of technically available devices and procedures to protect the privacy on the networks.

— The perpetual updating and upgrading of techniques for the protection of privacy on the networks techniques to counter the innovations in surveillance and intrusion techniques.

— To cure the effect of the immateriality and internationalization of the acts against the right of privacy, the criminalization and penalization of said acts should be tackled by describing the components of each crime in detail in an international model law or treaty describing each and every criminal act against the right of privacy and setting minimum requirements to be implemented in national legislations.

— The adoption of a model law pertaining to the protection of the right of privacy to be used as a model by sovereign states in their internal legislations in the quest for harmonizing the laws of different countries.

— The conflict of laws and the conflict of jurisdictions

should be settled by adopting enforceable international treaties.

— Extradition treaties should be entered into between sovereign states to facilitate the task of law enforcement and if they do exist they should be amended to cover cyber crimes.

— The penalization of the invasion of privacy with harsh physical penalties, financial fines, the judicial confiscation of the financial proceeds deriving from the act, the dissolution of the involved entity, in addition to administrative penalties and if the act is committed by a civil servant or one entrusted with the functioning and or operation of the network the sentence should be tougher, this also should be the case if the act is committed for financial gains. In addition to the penalty the aggressed party should have the right to receive full compensation for the damages.

— To state specifically in national legislations the nonprescription of the crimes and of the sentences penalizing the crimes against the Right of Privacy.

— The perpetual education of the legal practitioners involved in cyber crime including the legislators, the police officer, the prosecutor, the judge, and the lawyer with at least the minimum technical knowledge to understand the basic technical aspects of cyber crimes.

— To procure and provide law enforcement agencies with the technical capabilities to handle said crimes in the phases of investigation, enquiry, accusation, trial, and sentencing.

— The modification of the criminal procedural laws to adapt with the facts of cyber crime especially in the phases pertaining to the legal inspection of the networks, the apprehension and accusation of the perpetrator.

— The perpetual amendment of the laws protecting privacy on the networks to include any new material or immaterial evolution in the field of crimes against privacy.

— To finance law enforcement on the networks by levying a minimal tax on E. commerce and the use of confiscated financial proceeds deriving from cyber crimes.

— The propagation of utilitarian values arising the awareness of the importance of fair conduct and fair competition in the increase of the material gain and welfare for all the players.

— Last but not least, the practice of real democracy and transparency.

9

Ethical Problems of the Infoshpere

As the twentieth century draws to its end the creation of a global information infrastructure, a global information highway and a global stock of knowledge is seen as the key to building the information society of the twenty-first century. Once this has been completed the world is expected to become a 'global village', the advent of which was predicted by Professor M. McLuhan (Canada) in the early 1960s. This means that considerable changes can be expected in the relations between the people of different countries and nations, for—to take the metaphor of the 'global village' a little further—village as opposed to urban life is based on awareness of belonging to a particular community of people, one large family as it were, and of the resulting collective social responsibility. Village-dwellers know and understand one another well and resolve any difficulties arising among themselves collectively. Concurrently with the creation of the technological base of the 'global village', vigorous action is thus needed to remove the linguistic, cultural, educational and other barriers still dividing the peoples of the world into more or less hermetic ethno-cultural groups.

One of the best ways of doing this would be to eliminate the prejudices and stereotypes that create antagonistic 'we-and-they' relations. Such prejudices are inherent in all societies and their roots plunge deep into the history of humanity. 'We' are always good, noble, genuine people - which is just what the names of many still existing tribes and peoples mean - while 'they' are bad, treacherous, not genuine - enemies in short.

In the ancient world, the Greeks slapped the 'barbarian' label on any people whose language they did not understand and did not consider it worth their while to study. That kind of attitude, carrying as it does the connotation of cultural superiority, does nothing for that consolidation of humanity which is needed to overcome global problems. A major means of combating racial and cultural prejudice is a doctrine of the equivalence and complementarity of different cultures.

From this doctrine it follows that, for modern society, an ever more urgent issue is that of the preservation of the immense cultural heritage of the numerically smaller peoples, particularly those without written languages.

For this heritage reflects the age-old experience of peoples' interaction with nature and with one another. When a person who is a bearer of knowledge that has not been recorded in graphic form passes on, their knowledge too is gone for ever. Each such loss may be likened to the destruction of an entire library.

Many examples of such impoverishments of world culture could be given, but here we shall recount just one sad story.

The Taimyr peninsula in Siberia is home to the Nganasan, an ancient people who numbered approximately 900 in 1979. They call themselves 'nya', which means 'man'. The Nganasan have no written language. A few years ago the Nganasan storyteller Tubyaku Kosterkin lost his way and died in a blizzard. He was the sole repository of 40,000 legends, epic tales and songs, a significant contribution by this small but ancient nation to world culture. That cultural wealth was lost with the storyteller. Folklore specialists from the Institute of Philology of the Novosibirsk Scientific Centre of the Russian Academy of Sciences had succeeded in recording - and hence preserving for humanity - only a small part of that treasure.

UNESCO should give special attention to the problem of preserving the cultural heritage of small nations without written languages and organize systematic work in this respect (e.g. under a special programme).

It is important to be more respectful of the traditional ways of life of specific peoples and not thoughtlessly recast them in the mould of the so-called developed societies - which came into being in quite different geographical, historical and ideological conditions. With the best of intentions the Europeans did huge and irreparable damage to, for instance, the African peoples and the indigenous peoples of the Americas, destroying their traditional cultures. The essential requirement is the ability freely to communicate with other peoples and to understand their experience.

The warning given in the third report to the Club of Rome 'Reshaping the International Order' is still valid in this connection. The report was prepared by an international group of academics under the well-known Dutch economist and Nobel laureate Jan Tinbergen, and the warning, addressed to the developing countries, concerns the objectives and living standards of the Western countries: 'To conceive the objectives of development in terms of Western living standards may only compound confusion. The poor countries should reject the aim of imitating Western patterns of life. Development is not a linear process, and the aim of development is not to "catch up", economically, socially, politically or culturally.

Many aspects of Western life have become wasteful and senseless and do not contribute to peoples' real happiness. For the poor nations to attempt to imitate the rich may only mean that they trade one set of problems for another and in doing so discard or destroy much that is valuable in terms of their human resources and values'. It seems to us that this warning is quite in keeping with the present-day notion of sustainable development.

We know that to a considerable extent language determines how its vectors - people - see, apprehend and characterize the world around them (Sapir-Whorf hypothesis of linguistic relativity).

It is therefore important, for both cultural and historical reasons, that society should preserve and develop all languages. One of the latest registers gives the names, locations and variants of 6,170 living languages, excluding dialects, and shows how many people speak them. These people live in some 200 sovereign states.

Closely associated with the Sapir-Whorf hypothesis of linguistic relativity is the hypothesis that alphabetical (phonetic) writing was a key factor in the emergence of

Western theoretical science. This hypothesis was advanced by the Canadian physicist Robert K. Logan (University of Toronto) and formulated in his book 'The Alphabet Effect'.

Genuinely alphabetical writing, where 'alphabetical' is taken to mean an ordered aggregate of graphic symbols each of which signifies a single speech sound, was invented by the ancient Greeks in the eleventh to ninth centuries BC. The Greek alphabet is the basis for all European alphabets.

With the use of alphabetical writing, words expressing concepts and ideas are constructed from a very limited number of signs (letters) which may be repeated in the same word. Constant decomposition of words into their constituent elements - phonemes and letters - assisted the development of analytical reasoning, while the construction of words from those elements and the combination of words into sentences (statements) developed deductive reasoning, which provided the basis for formal logic and geometry. The alphabet made possible the development of classification and systematization, the art of analysis, and a new style of written exposition of thought - prose - without which theoretical science would be unthinkable.

Logan considers that the discovery and extension of the use of printing in Europe was closely bound up with alphabetical writing, although movable type was discovered at least four centuries earlier in China, where, however, it was not significantly developed. That may be because what became established in China was figurative, hieroglyphic writing based on special signs or characters signifying not elements of words but whole, indivisible concepts and ideas. A very large number of these different characters is thus needed to construct statements in Chinese, as many as there are concepts and ideas in fact, which means many thousands. The use of hieroglyphic writing was not conducive to the development of analytical thinking or theoretical science, although the world owes many major technical inventions to China (the compass, paper, gunpowder, iron smelting, etc.).

Logan's hypothesis is also linked to the functional asymmetry of the human brain. Most neurophysiologists and psychologists now agree that writing linear, alphabetical script occupies the brain's left hemisphere, while the right hemisphere specializes in the production of images, including hieroglyphic writing. They believe that the left hemisphere operates on a logical, analytical basis and the right in a figurative, synthetic manner. R. Ornstein identified the functions of the left hemisphere with the thinking of the rationalistic and technological West, and the functions of the right hemisphere with the thinking of the intuitive, mystic East.

This means that the peoples of the East, who use hieroglyphic writing, apparently apprehend and describe the world differently from the peoples of the West: they see the world as an integral (holistic) picture and not as a chaotic conglomeration of individual figures and colours. The cultural heritage of such peoples is therefore of huge value to humanity and deserving of preservation and study.

We believe that in a historical perspective the idea of the domination of the world community by any one language (e.g. English) has no future. The argument that in the Europe of the Middle Ages Latin served as the common language of science is not valid in this connection. It should not be forgotten that Latin was in fact a dead language, the language of books, and did not go against any specifically national style of communication or self-expression.

On the threshold of the new century it is interesting to recall H.G. Wells' analysis of the world prospects of various languages in his predictions for the present twentieth century.

'I do not think', he wrote in 1899, 'that any other language than these three [English, French and German] could hold out in the future. Italian may continue to thrive in the Po Valley, but only in conjunction with French. Spanish and Russian are strong languages but without a big enough reading public to become predominant, and what future can there be for a language without a reading public' I believe that these two languages are already doomed to exclusion. By the year 2000 all such languages will become secondary in bilingual countries alongside the predominant French or English and perhaps German, though this is less likely. Eastern Asia is still in a state of confusion as far as languages are concerned, but Chinese writing holds sway over all its dialects, and it is more than likely that this writing, moulded into a correct association of sounds, will become a world language'.

It is now clear that the great Englishman was wrong in his prognostications. But even if one agrees with his and many others' opinion that English may in time become the lingua franca of science and culture, it will be more than anything a new language that is based on present-day English, a jargon akin to pidgin English. We suspect that the English used nowadays in international organizations and at international meetings must grate ever more harshly on the ears of educated speakers of the real English.

In general, the interaction of national languages in the expanding international exchange of information poses a serious problem to which there is no easy solution. This question needs to be studied in greater depth, beginning with the compilation of a map of the languages used by modern science, technology and culture and the determination of the main trends and dynamics underlying changes to the map. The best-known investigation of this question remains the work of which an account was published by UNESCO in 1957. Acceptable ways of dealing with the problem of multilingualism in the infosphere might be:

- use of major languages (in terms of the number of speakers) for the purposes of scientific communication;
- development of retrieval systems in the different national languages in order to obtain access to world information resources;
- development of computer translation systems;
- teaching of the major languages in schools and on courses.

These major languages will probably for the time being have to serve as the media of communication on the global information network, including the Internet.

Ever greater problems are posed by the rapid growth in the quantity of information of every kind. Previously the main hope of dealing with the glut of information was seen to lie in the automation of information retrieval (IR) systems. Automated IR systems were created on the basis of age-old library and bibliographic principles. However, these systems are now of less and less help to researchers, engineers and managers in picking out the information they need. Almost any inquiry addressed through a modern automated IR system, with access to hundreds and thousands of databases, will result in an avalanche of information of variable quality, often repetitive, which the user is quite unable to apprehend or filter in a reasonable amount of time. A surplus of information, which in decision-making may be no less dangerous than too little information, is becoming increasingly common. Furthermore, users have begun to suffer from stress due to information overload which disorientates them and gives rise to a morbid state already termed 'information fatigue'.

To deal with growing information overload it is essential to devise more efficient methods of information retrieval making it possible to identify the content of documentary sources more clearly and eliminate at least those of them that contain secondary or recurring information. This could be achieved by intellectualizing information retrieval processes, i.e. studying and reproducing the corresponding mechanisms of human thought.

The creation of a new generation of information retrieval systems based on the utilization of knowledge is also important for the effective use of full-text databases and of numbered library holdings. Where such systems use multilingual databases, provision should be made for the possibility of interrogation, at least in any of the main natural languages.

This 'information overload', which calls for finer filtering and the enhancement of the information circulating in society, brings to mind the idea of creating a 'world brain' advanced by the great visionary and futurologist H.G. Wells in 1938. He imagined the 'world brain' as an immense clearing house that would handle all scientific and technological reports and other material. On the basis of such reports and material, the centre would prepare exhaustive and constantly updated encyclopaedias on the various branches of science. 'This', wrote H.G. Wells, 'would be a two-faceted organization, namely a collection of information that was continually being digested and condensed and, in addition, a publication and distribution system. It would be a distribution centre for universities and scientific research establishments, serving as the cortex for these ganglia'.

Clearly, in the late 1930s the idea of creating such a 'world brain' belonged to the realm of science fiction, since the necessary technological resources did not yet exist. But now the idea can be looked on as a practical proposition.

Until printing was discovered, people could only study with the aid of their memory. 'Reason ever and in all things resorts to memory', observed Blaise Pascal in his time. With the advent of books, however, the dissemination of knowledge and instruction became considerably less dependent on memory. But instruction, the gathering of essential information and decision-making all the same required the recollection and comprehension of facts and ideas, the search for analogies, and so on, namely a certain mental agility. With databases, personal computers and high-speed data transmission, however, there is less need for personal study of any given subject since existing information on it can be rapidly obtained via the computer. It becomes pointless to commit anything to memory. But if information never settles in the long-term human memory it is not analysed, and this is absolutely essential for its logical processing. Non-interpreted or misinterpreted information can only result in superficial conclusions, at best. It follows that modern information technology may have a negative, as well as a positive, effect on the dissemination and assimilation of knowledge and also on the quality of decision-making.

Another factor is that people now acquire an ever greater part of their knowledge from visual images (their processing in the human brain, as already noted, takes place mainly in the right hemisphere) and not in the form of language, processed in the brain's left hemisphere. People read less and less and look at more and more television and computer images. It is possible that this may adversely affect the intellectual development of humanity. In our opinion, these issues deserve close attention and serious study.

A whole set of problems has also arisen concerning the legal and ethical aspects of the presentation and utilization of information. The development and application of electronic means of data input, storage, retrieval and dissemination are having the effect of dismantling the traditional system of written (printed) communication. This primarily concerns books and periodicals, which over the past 300 years have been the main vehicle for the dissemination of scientific research findings and cultural works. Mechanisms for dealing with a set of complex problems have been devised and are applied in the preparation of books and scientific journals. Scientific journals do not normally put into circulation material that falls short of generally accepted criteria, as contributions are read through first. Being issued in hundreds and thousands of copies, books and periodicals are a useful means of recording and confirming the priority given to their authors. They also make for the development and use of unified scientific and cultural terminology, and so forth. And the electronic variants with which we are now provided cannot as yet fully replace the printed word. The problem of electronic books and periodicals is crucial to the further development of science and culture, requiring careful and specialized study.

The information society of the twenty-first century will require the careful preservation of national attainments in science, culture and language and the elaboration of new mechanisms of international communication in the infosphere, using computerized systems for the retrieval and translation of information, ensuring universal access to the global stock of knowledge. As the matters under consideration are of worldwide significance, it would be appropriate for their study and development to be undertaken under the auspices of UNESCO and the International Council of Scientific Unions, as was done, for instance, in the mid-1960s for assessment of the primary periodical editions in the realm of the physical sciences (Boutry Commission) and for the feasibility study leading to the establishment of the World Science Information System (UNISIST programme).

10

Data Accessibility and the Digtal Divide

A pre-requisite for citizen access to government data is that the government first makes that data available to citizens. On this, different governments have taken different views, some of which create access barriers. These views can be represented as lying anywhere within a triangle between three extremes.

— *Data is a public asset.* Public sector data is seen as owned by everyone since it has been gathered about and from everyone, often compulsorily. The view here is that data should, in general, be made freely available as it can assist both social and economic development. At most, a charge should be levied that merely reflects the cost of output and transmission. Citizens have a right to see the data held about them and other public sector data, with certain exceptions.

— *Data is a private asset.* Public sector data is seen as owned by the department which owns the computer on which that data resides. The view here is that the public sector has invested money in producing data which often has considerable commercial value. Data should therefore be sold at the highest possible price to earn valuable revenue for the public sector. Citizens may see the data about themselves and some other items of data so long as they pay.

— *Data is not an asset.* Data is not seen as important enough to warrant open consideration of issues of ownership, value and charging. Where used, data is virtually a personal asset of particular public sector staff. Data is not generally made available and citizens do not have rights of access, except perhaps through 'under the counter' payments.

Different governments take different viewpoints. At the federal level, the US government thinks 'public asset'. There is no copyright on federal government data and, by law, that data must be made accessible for the marginal cost of distribution. A recent global survey indicated that more than three-quarters of national governments followed this view, at least for online data (Zammit 2000).

By contrast, a number of US states think 'private asset'. So, too, does the UK central government with guidelines 'encouraging agencies to maximise income by charging what the market will bear' (POST 1998:32). Others favour a mixed approach. The European Commission takes the line that:

"Pricing policies may vary depending on the nature of the information. A price should be established which reflects the costs of preparing and passing it on to the private sector, but which does not necessarily include the full cost of routine administration. The price may be reduced if provision of the resulting information service is deemed to be necessary in the public interest."

These different views will present differing hurdles to accessibility: very low barriers under a 'public asset' regime; much higher barriers under a 'private asset' regime. Growth of the Internet and its 'data must be free' philosophy may favour the 'public asset' view. It certainly leads to the absurd situation in which the UK government tries to sell internationally-shared data, such as that from observation satellites, for hundreds of dollars per item when that same data can be downloaded free of charge from US agency Web sites.

As well as these practical grounds, the 'private asset' view is also being questioned from the perspective of national interest: "You get a few pennies in, but how much do you lose in potential gains in society by not allowing information to be passed on more cheaply?

Further barriers may exist to making data available *electronically*. In the UK, for instance:

— "Many of the operations of government are still paper based. ...

— Even where information is stored electronically, there may be a need to collate and process data manually (e.g. because of lack of interoperability between different data systems).

— There is no mandate or framework to make data available electronically: many officials may be unaware of this option, leaving electronic publishing as a secondary activity of IT or other personnel rather than a primary component of a department's communications philosophy."

Failure to properly control electronic data in government can equally lead to a backlash against availability. In 1999, for example, the Pentagon closed down many of its

.mil Web sites having discovered those sites had made electronically available:

"a treasure trove of information, including the maintenance status of fighter aircraft engines, air refueling schedules, an Air Force 'how-to' manual for determining targets to attack, and army manuals on small unit tactics and the use of many weapons. ... The director of the Defense Intelligence Agency claimed threats to security no longer come from spies and moles but from simply releasing too much informatio". Whether misguided or realistic, any backlash may mean that 'the golden age of public access to government information on the Internet is over.'

Technology and Other Access Resources

If citizens can overcome the first hurdle – of having government data made available – they must then have the resources necessary to access that data. Some important access resources are rarely discussed. They include:

— *Money/time*: it costs money and time to access government data. Whilst people tend to have increasing amounts of the former, they have decreasing amounts of the latter.

— *Knowledge*: citizens can only access available data if they know the data exists, that it is available, and how it can be accessed. It would be fair to say that the vast majority of citizens in all countries do not possess this knowledge in relation to all public sector data. Vast swathes of government data remain untapped by huge numbers of citizens simply because they have no idea that it is there or how to get hold of it.

— *Motivation*: citizens must want to access public sector data. Public servants often assume a great thirst for government data exists among the general public, and they suppose that, if only those citizens were given access, they would drink down data by the gallon. In practice, many public information systems are marked less by the enthusiasm of a minority of citizens than by the apathy and disinterest of the majority. Most citizens of Western nations hardly care what government is doing. Presented with the Internet, they will follow their main interests of sex, shopping and entertainment rather than details of the latest local government enterprise zone scheme.

The most-discussed aspect of data accessibility is information technology (IT). Why? Because, unlike the other resources, it is sexy and tangible. However, IT is very much a two-edged sword as regards access to government data. On the one hand it reduces barriers. Compare downloading a government report via the Internet with going out to buy a paper version.

IT has made it far cheaper, quicker and easier to access that data. A wealth of data that, because of the barriers, was essentially inaccessible in paper form becomes accessible when it turns digital. Citizens can also re-use the data more easily because it arrives in electronic form. And a good search engine will reduce knowledge barriers though, as noted, motivational barriers are unlikely to be affected.

The foregoing represents the technological 'good news'. On the downside, IT raises barriers and has created a *digital divide* across which one group reaps the benefits of IT-enabled accessibility and one group cannot. The skills required for accessing manually-held information are little more than literacy. For IT-based data, computer literacy must also be added and not everyone has those skills. Just as important are the issues of cost and ownership.

Accessing individual items may be cheaper with IT, but to get that far you need an IT infrastructure in place first – a computer, a network connection, software, and so on. That all costs money whereas, by comparison, actually reading paper-based materials costs nothing.

Because of those costs, there is a very uneven profile of those who own and use IT: the rich not the poor; the graduate not the school leaver; the ethnic majority not the ethnic minority; the urban not the rural citizen; the young not the old; men not women. In the mid-1990s, for example, of more than 100,000 daily recipients of White House electronic documents, 85% were under 50, 80% were male, and 50% had a postgraduate qualification (*Infosys* 1994).

Since that time, general access levels have increased markedly. Several US cities recorded more than half of all adults having access to the Web by the end of 1999 (*Government Technology* 1999). Within this overall increase, the number of women, seniors, ethnic minority members, etc. has also increased.

This is all to be expected. The penetration curves for IT are following very similar – possibly faster and steeper – patterns to those carved out by earlier technologies like the telephone and television. However, whilst absolute numbers of previously-excluded groups are rising, inequalities persist and one must constantly push behind the averages to find the realities of access. 125 years after the invention of the telephone, half the world's population has yet to make a phone call. Even in Western nations, one-quarter of the poorest 20% of households does not have a phone.

Access gaps hold equally for the Internet. The digital divide still runs nationally. In the US, for example.

— High-income urban households are 20 times more likely to have home Internet access than low-income rural households.

— Low-income white families are three times more likely to have home Internet access than equivalent black families; four times more likely than equivalent Hispanic families.

— Those without disabilities are three times more likely to have home Internet access than those with disabilities.

And the digital divide still runs internationally – there are more Internet account holders in London than in the whole of Africa, and many of the latter are rich, white, urban South Africans.

Of course, one must equally take care with even these figures. Poor households and poor communities often share technologies in a way that richer ones do not. In Africa, for example, Western models of one email/ Internet account serving one individual do not hold. Instead, the typical account owner is an intermediary who shares access with an estimated five to ten others through networks of family, friends or colleagues. However, whilst moderating the impact of inequality, these modes of operation do not remove an inequality that sees the majority of the world's population cut off from computers and the Internet. If 200 million people worldwide used the Internet in 2000, that leaves 5,800 million – more than 96% of the world's population – who did not.

Governments are generally well aware of the dangers of IT strengthening the 'social exclusion' that prevents some citizen groups from fulfilling their economic and social potential.

A variety of initiatives are therefore in place that try to overcome the ownership and use inequalities described above. These aim not just to increase access to government data but also to bring other perceived benefits of access to IT: access to IT-related skills, access to employment information, access to lower-cost online shopping, etc.

Some initiatives have focused on *increasing ownership*. For example, in 1997, the Israeli government set up a five-year social inclusion fund of c. US$50m which is purchasing home PCs for an estimated 30,000 poor families. Other governments have used tax breaks or subsidies as ways to try to increase the numbers of those who actually own IT.

Ownership initiatives can only go so far and, for many, the costs of personal ownership will remain prohibitive. For these groups, governments may set up initiatives focused on *increasing access* to IT that is government- or community-owned IT. Such IT may be placed in a variety of locations:

— Public spaces, such as common areas within shopping malls.

— Semi-public spaces, such as libraries or sport facilities.

— Dedicated spaces, such as community telecentres housing a room-full of Internet-linked PCs.

Such placement of IT only addresses technology barriers, not skill barriers. For some, the skill barriers mean they require the assistance of an *IT intermediary* through whom the citizen indirectly accesses the new IT infrastructure, including electronic public data. Alternatively, they may require an *IT facilitator* who will train them or help them to gain access themselves. These roles may be informal, such as the public librarian who takes time to assist clients, or they may be formal, such as the telecentre worker whose job it is to bring community members online.

Despite all these measures, however, IT inequalities do and will remain. The watchword for government must therefore be 'supplement' not 'supplant'. Provision of public sector data and other services electronically should be seen as an additional weapon in the armoury that sits alongside paper-based or face-to-face methods. It should not be seen as way of replacing those more traditional methods.

Unfortunately, cost-cutting pressures in government mean such principles can easily forgotten. As so often with technological change, it will then be the poor and disadvantaged who find they have gained last and gained least from the new technology.

Recognising some (though not all) of the barriers identified above, and in a bid to ensure access to data across the public sector (and beyond) some governments have introduced *freedom of information* (FOI) legislation. In the US, for example the Freedom of Information Act was introduced in 1966, amended in 1996 by the Electronic Freedom of Information Act, which guarantees public access to most federal government data electronically.

These Acts – at least in theory – enshrine the 'public asset' viewpoint in law and have resulted in about 400,000 requests for access per year. To help with this access, government information locator services have been set up that identify, describe and assure access to such data.

The particular content of FOI legislation varies from country to country. In Ireland, for example:

"The Freedom of Information Act, 1997, was the first significant piece of legislation that obliged government Departments and Offices to publish details of their information holdings. This Act asserts the right of members of the public to obtain access to official information to the greatest extent possible consistent with the public interest and the right to privacy.

Under the Act, public bodies are required to make public certain information about themselves and also to make available details of their internal rules, procedures, interpretations, etc. used in decision making. Many Departments and Offices publish this information on the Internet. The central purpose of this information is to assist the public in ascertaining the information held by each organisation and how to access it.

In respect of non-personal information, fees may be charged in respect of the time spent in efficiently locating and retrieving records, based on a standard hourly rate. Photocopying charges may also apply. In respect of personal records, copying charges only will apply, save where a large number of records are involved. No charges may apply in respect of the time spent by public bodies in considering requests.

Some countries go further. Those in Scandinavia provide a public right of access to all documents kept by a public authority, including electronic documents.

However, this positive picture of facilitated access for citizens is not widely found. Only just over a quarter of governments worldwide have freedom of information legislation and in many cases it is hedged with exemptions which may include:

· "exemptions in the interest of the state, for example relating to national security, public order, economic interests, international relations, legislative procedures, etc. ...

- exemptions in the interest of third parties, for example relating to privacy, intellectual property, commercial secrets, judicial procedures, etc.
- exemptions to protect the decision making process, for example preliminary or 'internal use' of information, etc.
- exemptions to avoid unreasonable costs or workload in the administrations concerned, for example information already published or excessive requests."

The growing pattern of exemptions has been seen in the US. A door that was opened by the 1966 legislation and its 1974 amendment has been constantly nudged closed by subsequent legislation and court decisions. These moves have mainly involved greater protection for law enforcement agency records and for personal privacy at the expense of openness.

The overall impact of FOI for citizens seems limited:

"FOI is used mainly by business to obtain commercial information in Canada and the United States. In Norway and Denmark, it is used mainly by the press. ... In general, FOI does not appear to have been a very potent instrument in the hands of the public to promote greater transparency and participation. Indirectly, however, the threat of its use appears to have caused some greater degree of disclosure, though it has also led to greater use of oral discussion and decision-making, and in some cases the actual alteration or destruction of documents.".

Thus, whilst legislation is a positive move in theory; in practice, it has not yet fulfilled its potential.

Citizen access to government data is recognised to bring both economic and social benefits. Yet there are many roadblocks along the path to access. The very first requirement – availability of government data – can be problematic. Governments face the tension of new public management, torn between the public service ethos of providing data for free, and the neo-liberal ethos of charging what the market will bear. The former does not always win out. Nor, despite all the talk of 'eGovernment' have public sector procedures yet caught up with the potential for electronic data provision.

In relation to access, a number of barriers exist. Freedom of Information legislation has attempted to bring down some legislative barriers, but the self-preserving, sometimes self-serving instincts of governments have neutered many such initiatives. Governments have been rather better at recognising technological access barriers, but the scale of the task means current projects are but drops in the ocean. And governments have been poor at recognising some of the less tangible access barriers, such as knowledge and motivation.

They seem to have been worse still at recognising that even if all the access barriers identified above could be overcome, they represent only the first step in the process since they merely present the data to the citizen. Many other resources are needed if that data is to be turned into information and if that information is then to be applied for citizen learning, decisions and actions:

— *Data into information.* Data remains data unless citizens have the skills and expertise to turn it into information. In particular, they need the knowledge: to assess whether the data is truth or lies, of value or not; and to apply that data by adapting it to their particular needs and circumstances. Many disadvantaged citizen groups lack such knowledge.

— *Information into action.* Information about new government tax rules is of no value if you cannot afford to pay tax. Information about a government decision that may damage your community is of no value if you lack the money, time, motivation or power to challenge that decision. Information about new employment opportunities is of no value if you lack the skills or knowledge to take up those opportunities. Barriers to resources for action therefore constrain citizens even if they can access information.

A model is therefore needed, as shown in Figure 2, that takes understanding beyond just access issues to the whole chain of steps that turn government data into citizen action.

The model is a reminder of the steps and barriers that citizens face in making use of government data. It is also a reminder that disadvantaged citizens will remain disadvantaged because of inequalities in a broad range of resource endowments – knowledge, skills, money, power and others – regardless of whether they can access data using IT. At best, then, access to data and access to IT might be necessary but they far from sufficient conditions to enable effective citizen use of government data.

11

Ethical Framework: Mechanisms for User Enabled Choice

To quote from UNESCO, "The goal of the UNESCO INFOethics programme is to stimulate reflection and debate on the ethical, legal and societal aspects of the Information Society." This chapter investigates a set of mechanisms for user enabled choice and normative claims on the Internet. If there is a constant in the short history of the Internet, it is the technological symbol of the post-modern culture of the late twentieth century, in which unified authorities give way to multiple stakeholders with complex and contradictory agendas. A tradition of decentralized participation in the creation of socio-technical systems recognizes the encouraged individual user to add new content and tools to the system as a whole—the unified operating authority is replaced by a contradictory, and even chaotic form of control. Structural and systemic elements, such as web filtering systems, will be examined for they represent acknowledged conditions to uphold freedom of expression through choice mechanisms. If the Internet is to continue as an innovative means of collaboration, discovery, and social interaction, it will need to build upon its adaptability and participatory design.

It is perhaps worthwhile to quote from a recent European Union communication:

In social terms, the Internet represents significant potential benefits. It offers unprecedented opportunities for empowering citizens, and for connecting them to ever richer sources of digital information. The Internet has been used by great effect in a number of Member States to connect administrations and citizens. Lowering the barriers of entry to the dissemination of information on the local, as well as on the global scale, the Internet allows individuals or associations to publish information about their activities to a wide audience at modest cost. In the field of culture, the Internet already contributes significantly to the creation and dissemination of European digital multimedia content, fostering linguistic diversity, and the rayonnement of European cultures in the world. As exemplified by a number of innovative projects linking libraries, schools and universities in Europe, the Internet is similarly the key to a new "electronic literacy", and, as such, the cornerstone of the new and far-reaching European Union initiative, the Action Plan "Learning in the Information Society ".

Having stated this, like any other communication technology, the Internet carries an amount of potentially harmful or illegal content and it can be misused as a vehicle for criminal activities. Although there is not widespread 'misuse' of the Internet, a variety of distinct areas are impacted upon. These are covered by different legal regimes and instruments at the national and international level, e.g., national security (instructions on bomb-making, illegal drug production, terrorist activities); protection of minors (abusive forms of marketing, violence, pornography); protection of human dignity (incitement to racial hatred or racial discrimination); economic security (fraud, instructions on pirating credit cards); information security (malicious hacking); protection of privacy (unauthorised communication of personal data, electronic harassment); protection of reputation (libel, unlawful comparative advertising); intellectual property (unauthorised distribution of copyrighted works, e.g. software or music).

While the benefits of the Internet far outweigh its negative aspects, there are issues of public, political, commercial and legal interest which must be addressed. Reflecting these concerns, recent political discussions in the European Union have stressed the need for urgent action and concrete solutions.

While ethical discussions certainly cannot provide answers to all the technical constraints presented by the nature of the Internet, they do offer a normative orientation and facilitate the dialogue with a concerned public. There are many specific technical mechanisms deserving attention. One such mechanism activates Internet Service Providers (ISPs) in a new form, for they have the option to provide users with the choice to control the content delivered to users over the Internet.

Rather than retrieving items from the Web, filtering systems are used to selectively restrict access to materials on the Web. Such systems may be used to 'filter out' Web sites or Web pages that contain material that is objectionable to a community of users. Such systems could be used to restrict access by users to sites containing pornographic material or hate material.

Measures that promote the following principles:

Communication Principle

- The right of communications as a fundamental human right

Free Expression Principle

- States should promote the right to free expression and the right to receive information regardless of frontiers.

If users have the choice to control the content delivered to them, a social origin of conduct has been created. The momentum of large-scale sociotechnical systems, such as codes of conduct, offer a hierarchical framework of interpretation of conduct. Alfred D. Chandler in The Visible Hand a monumental study of modern enterprise, presents documentation to defend the hypothesis that the construction and day-to-day operation of many technical systems in the nineteenth and twentieth centuries require the development of a particular social form - a large-scale hierarchical organization administered by powerful agents. Chandler points to ways in which technologies 'demand' or 'require' this form of human association. The only conceivable arrangements made possible by the nature of the Internet of power and authority are those of decentralized, democratic user self-management. The interesting question, however, has to do with whether or not this pattern is in any sense a requirement of such systems, especially a system such as the Internet.

The matter ultimately rests on judgment and interpretation of the steps which are necessary in the workings of protecting human dignity in the digital age. Was Plato right in saying that a ship at sea needs steering by a decisive hand and that this could only be accomplished by a single captain and an obedient crew? The captain exists through user empowerment. In the content area, this translates to providing users with the means to control content in their own homes.

If political language for evaluating and accommodating information technology includes only categories having to do with tools and uses, if it does not include attention to the meaning of the mechanisms of filters. Monitoring of codes of conduct prove to be most intractable, they demonstrate the significance of the entrenched interests that have guided technological and social choices and development made early on in the innovation of the Internet. Information Technology has not only been representative of investment through structure, but investment by users of conduct and skills. To integrate codes of conduct would not only shoot down the expected social investment on the Internet but also threaten the interests and integrity of the users. A symbolic demonstration of user enabled choices must be demonstrated in order to promote answers to imperative questions: Whose strategy? Whose choice? During this time of process innovation codes of conduct, the realities, significance and consequences of barriers to access, whether publicly or privately created must be explored.

Social choice arguments provide a partial depiction of the process through which technological choices are made and implemented. John Child in Organization Structure, Environment and Performance: The Role of Strategic Choice portrays strategic choice, and strategy formation in general, as an interpretive process by organizational leaders. What distinguishes those leaders, however, is the power they possess to enact their interpretations as plans and directives that structure the organization. In this sense Child makes an important and very relevant point: the behavior of organizational leaders is as likely to be affected by broadly normative, ideological, and political considerations as is that of any other organizational or group member. In this formulation he builds into the concept of strategic choice a conception of politics that goes well beyond simple self-interest to include distinctive perspectives or beliefs about how people and organizations 'should' work. Given this conceptual base, rooted in a strategic choice perspective is a mediating role of organizational process and politics in relation to technological choice. The value of social choice perspective resides in its insistence on the inclusion of social and organizational context as mainstays in the analysis of technological change.

The explicit attention to the active role that peer-to-peer socio-technical relations will play in influencing, if not directly determining strategic choice initiatives. Essentially, peer-to-peer communications takes away the ISP as the middleman. Therefore, the only filtering technologies that would apply would be black and white lists in the browser, label processing in the browser and restricted access at the server.

This is important because it would mean that the government could not impose filtering at the ISP level. However, it also means that we could not stop people accessing sites that teach them how to build bombs. Technology is always a two-edged sword.

As explained by Oram: "In various ways [peer-to-peer communications] return content, choice, and control to ordinary users. Tiny end points on the Internet, sometimes without even knowing each other, exchange information and form communities. There are no more clients and servers -- or at least, the servers retract themselves discreetly. Instead, the significant communication takes place between cooperating peers. And thus, starting around early July 2000, the new Internet model was dubbed peer-to-peer."

Technology partnered with normative claims uncovers and furthers fields where ethical problems have not been previously raised. An attempt to clarify both the legal framework and the current practices of the industry continues.

Filtering methods

The question is not how to use technology to enforce legal statutes (countries have laws for defining what is legal and what is not) but rather as a way to ensure, as much as possible, that unintentional access to possibly legal, but nonetheless objectionable material, is minimized, particularly for children. There is an array of technological approaches available that can be deployed both at the Internet Service Provider (ISP) level and at the home or school level. It is the control mechanisms that ISPs have the option to provide and the control mechanisms that users can choose to utilize, that was the subject a report by two of the current authors. There are a variety of types of control mechanisms available described below.

ISP control mechanisms have significant promise in providing content management, especially if they place some control in the hands of users. These mechanisms provide a more technologically robust system upon which parents can place greater reliance than on desktop filters. Although desktop filtering technologies may be more prone to tampering, they empower users to control the content at a finer level than would be expected from an ISP. These technologies, however, are not 100% effective in that they can be circumvented by computer-adept people. They cannot be relied upon to effectively filter all undesirable content and they may filter out some desirable content unintentionally. Nevertheless, these technologies provide an important part of the user's content-control tool kit. Whether the control is managed remotely at the ISP or locally on the desktop, transparency and knowledge of the mechanisms deployed is important. Users need to understand what is being filtered, when it is being filtered, and why it is being filtered.

The premise behind such filtering is that it is better, particularly for young children, to miss some material than to get offensive material, i.e., precision is more important than recall. However, filtering mechanisms are difficult to maintain in an environment in which new material is constantly being added and new Web technologies continue to be developed. To operate effectively, filtering systems must acquire and maintain, over the long term, accurate knowledge not only about the users but also about the Web sites and Web pages.

Overview of Core Technologies and Application Classification

There are a number of ways that access to content on the Internet can be controlled, and these rely on one or more underlying core technologies. Applications typically combine core technologies and can be situated at the ISP, at the client, or both. To date, there is no clear recommendation as to the best method or even where it is best applied. There is no "silver bullet" here. Nonetheless, the users must be informed of their options and risks and, where feasible, involved in the process.

The core technologies include the following:

- *Site labels.* Labeling refers to schemes to assign content related labels to URLs and/or specific Web pages. Individual rating protocols exist, in general, separate from products or applications using these ratings. Once a label schema has been chosen by a service or a community, then a language, such as PICS (Platform for Internet Content Selection) is required to implement that schema for individual Web pages. In general, these labels can be stored as part of the Web page or separately from the Web page in a database. Labels may be the result of self-rating, third-party authority rating, or community rating by interested users.

- *Lists of appropriate or inappropriate sites ("white" and "black lists").* The most frequently used content control mechanism is the use of lists of acceptable and/or unacceptable URLs. "White" lists are used to define a domain of "safe" Web sites within which users can browse. These typically require people to search and select sites that are approved by the provider of the list. "Black" lists are lists compiled of URLs from which requests will not be serviced. In almost all cases the lists are compiled by people either working alone or as communities of raters.

- *Automated text analysis.* Another way to analyze a Web site is to use software that scans the text of a site to determine the relevance or suitability of pages. Users or groups of users have profiles of interests (positive and/or negative), consisting of keywords and phrases, that are used in this determination. Almost all content based filtering uses some variation of keyword matching, where keywords from a profile of interest are compared against the keywords occurring in the content of the specific Web page. Text analysis is also used to screen search terms from search queries.

- *Authorization.* Encryption, password protection, and credit card validation techniques are used to authenticate that a user has the authorization to access given services or data. These techniques are described further below.
- *Activity tracing.* Internet usage can be traced by using the server log files and other data logs. These files store details of all Web accesses and can be used to analyze web-related activities.

The types of content control applications that are built on these underlying technologies include the following:

- *Special purpose browsers for children.* Browser applications, such as SurfMonkey, can be written that are targeted to child users. Such applications can provide easier search strategies and friendlier graphics, remove advertisements, and provide filtering and search-safe domains in a way that makes it transparent to the user.
- *Child-friendly search engines and portals.* The idea behind both special purpose child-friendly search engines and portals is to use a third party gateway to Web content. Child-friendly portals, such as Yahooligans are Web access sites that try to provide a domain of safe sites for the user to explore. As long as the user comes in through the portal, they view a

pre-selected domain set of the Web.

- *Proxy applications.* Application software can be added to server proxy modules that permit the execution of text analysis and URL list comparisons on every Internet browser request and response.
- *Activity monitors.* Rather than restrict or control access to Web sites proactively, these applications monitor and log Internet activity for parental review. Software is also available to ensure the protection of the identity of children as users of the Internet.
- *Restricted access applications.* Applications residing on the host site can be written that restrict access to services or data on that site to authorized users. Data may be encrypted so that only authorized users can decrypt and view the data. Login names and passwords may be assigned to authorized users of sites with restricted data. A host site may require a user to provide a valid credit card number or some other proof of age authority before allowing access to the site. New biometric algorithms and hardware devices are being developed to uniquely identify users using, for example, finger scanning, retina scanning, and voice print, and user's individual typing rhythm .
- *Non-HTTP applications.* Applications can be written using these core technologies to control content of email and to control access to ftp sites, telnet hosts, discussion and chat groups, and newsgroups. Email filtering applications focus on email spam (flood of copies of messages) and email content filtering. Spam filtering uses rules to scan the headers of incoming messages to eliminate likely spam messages. Content filtering is a finer grained inspection of the message

contents, typically using a profile of keywords. For more control, email applications, such as Email for Kids give the parent control over both incoming and outgoing messages. News server filtering, such as for UseNet, is largely accomplished using two core technologies: lists of acceptable/not-acceptable newsgroups to block at the newsgroup level, and keyword based filtering. FTP (file transfers) can be controlled by preventing any ftp access, controlling the sites, or the use of user id and password. Since telnet is remote access of a user to his or her own account on a remote computer, the main control mechanism available is disallowing telnet access at a firewall. Controlling access to discussion groups, chat rooms, and instant-messaging applications is generally achieved by using access lists. Often these control features are bundled with other control features in broader applications such as NetNanny or SurfMonkey.

Potential of the Core Technologies

All of these core technologies have a role to play in control mechanisms for the Web. None of these core technologies provides a long-term solution in its own. Systems will need to combine the technologies in innovative ways to provide effective solutions within well-defined contexts:

- *Site labeling systems* are the most flexible and perhaps hold the most promise for the future. Labels may be generated by the content provider, third party rating services, communities of users, or individual users. Software at the ISP and/or client then uses the labels that have been assigned. Questions arise as to the completeness of label coverage in a billion-page Web domain and the quality of labels, i.e., who generates them and who guarantees them.

- *URL lists* are the most effective in controlling domains of access. This method is particularly good for creating child-friendly sites. However, the use of lists does not provide the flexibility of labels and the Web is growing so quickly it is very hard to keep lists up-to-date and accurate.
- *Content Filtering* by automated analysis of the content of Web sites is problematic at best, due to the vagaries of natural language, the difficulties of cross-language filtering, and the difficulties of determining the content of graphics and images. Although using this technology to assist in the labeling of sites based on text categorization techniques does hold some promise.
- *Access authorization* can be effective as a reverse filter, restricting who can have access to a given site, yet many problems, both technical and non-technical remain. Encryption schemes, such as PKI (Public Key Infrastructure) or Private Key Algorithms require the client to be in possession of a valid key in order for the decryption to occur. Users wishing to access data or transfer data sites with user ids and passwords must first obtain these and then keep them. The use of credit cards or proof of age cards over the Internet is problematic at best. Clearly many people over 18 do not have credit cards and there then exists the need to assure that the user is the actual owner of the credit or proof of age card. Australia , for example, has proposed the use of credit card validation to

verify that a person requesting access to adult material is 18 years of age or older. There is a real concern over privacy with the application of this technique within Australia.

- *Activity tracing monitors* what has been done, rather than actually filter out any material. Issues of privacy must be addressed as well.
- *Non-HTTP applications* rely generally on lists of blocked or accepted sites, keyword filters, and user ids and passwords. As noted above, none of these techniques works particularly well. The access control concerns with Discussion Groups, Chat Groups, and ICQ center on the appropriateness of the community of users of the particular group.

It must be emphasized that none of the above technologies is 100% effective and that the content of the Web is, by its very nature, volatile. In order to be (more) effective, these technologies have to be used in combination and in layers, both at the ISP and client. For instance, a combination of labels and URL lists can be used at the ISP in conjunction with a final filter using local lists and/or automated analysis techniques at the client.

In general, content control mechanisms can be applied proactively or reactively. These mechanisms are not disjoint with respect to whether applied in a proactive or reactive manner, but the application philosophy differs. ISPs and third party authorities are more likely to be able to provide proactive services while ISPs and clients are more likely use the reactive mechanisms. Proactive or pre-search control mechanisms refer to pre-search result activities that collect information that may be used to prevent the retrieval of inappropriate

Web pages or to define domains of appropriate Web sites for communities of users. Proactive control mechanisms include: the creation, storage, and use of labels, and the creation of lists of good and bad URLs. Both labels and URL lists require significant investment in resource identification and the discovery of both suitable and unsuitable sites. Reactive or post-search control refers to the analysis of URL domain names, metadata, or content after a Web search has been executed. Post search control mechanisms may also use URL lists and assessment of label information associated with a given page. In addition, post search may use a content based filtering technique to analyze the actual content of pages returned by the search and on that basis allow or restrict access to pages.

While virtually all of these techniques can be implemented by an ISP, it is important that use of filtering be transparent to the user community. The user should understand what is being filtered, when it is being filtered, and why it is being filtered. The potential for shared and informed Web content filtering has not yet been realized and a co-operative approach of policy and technology will be needed to meet that goal.

In spite of the above-mentioned filtering mechanisms, the following issues remain to be addressed.

Freedom of expression

The first and most important principle for the freedom of expression.

Various legal consequences appear to be:

- Most ISPs are responsible for the content that they

produce and place online in their name.

- As Internet users may freely express themselves on the Internet, they are responsible for their own behaviour.
- ISPs, who are not responsible for the content placed online by their own users, expect them to respect their General Terms.
- In practice, personal pages, which may be changed at any time by the author, cannot reasonably be the object of the systematic and exhaustive control by ISPs on their contents, their rights, and their links to other sites. Through reports provided by users, ISPs have the capability of detecting litigious contents, and remove them according to their General Terms.
- ISPs are not the authors or editors of content produced and placed on line by third parties.
- Within newsgroups (which are unmoderated spaces for public discussion) ISPs do not have the means to prevent the creation of discussion groups which they do not initiate. Therefore, their secondary involvement can only be after the appearance of illegal discussion groups. ISPs may block the spread of discussion groups that do not conform to their General Terms of Use or upon judicial injunction. However, the filtered groups may remain accessible from other access providers abroad.

Protection of minors

Some countries address the protection of minors from harmful content in their codes of conduct, promoting best practices such as ensuring that content which is unlawful or impermissible. Certain other countries address this concern mainly through co-operation with public authorities or private organisations that run hotlines.

Codes of conduct have in common the same coercive mean, which is the expulsion of a member. However, the filtering systems identified above indicate the following:

From a technical perspective, the removal of content can only be obtained from :

- the author or
- the hosting ISP.

From a legal perspective, removal of content can be obtained from:

- the author,
  - on its own initiative or
  - following advice of a non judiciary organisation,
- the hosting ISP, according to
  - its General Terms, or
  - the judiciary authority assessing the law, or
  - the law enforcement authority as is the case on child pornography in Belgium and United-Kingdom)

In fact, expulsion is the only legitimate way for a non-judiciary organisation to persuade its members to respect a code of conduct.

Filtering harmful activity or content on the Internet can be technically designed only after normative standards are adopted. Increasingly, it is recognized that the existence of offensive online content - albeit a very small portion of the available online content - may be a significant barrier to the growth and development of universal access to the Internet. In this chapter normative claims and filtering mechanisms have been presented to facilitate approaches of governments, business and civil society in ensuring security, privacy protection and freedom of expression on global information networks. The Internet demands responsibility as much as it offers freedom.

Although codes of conduct are rooted in national contexts, multi-national Internet industry associations share common principles, such as freedom of expression, protection of minors, data protection. They also share common procedures such as expulsion of a member who does not conform with their code of conduct. Understanding the efficiency and the limits of the current codes will allow to build on the common principles already defined. Although it does not answer all questions the European Union 'green paper' on the protection of minors and human dignity is worthy of further examination and development.

International instruments related to human rights recognize the necessity of concerted and balanced effort for drafting of strategies for the development, evaluation, and maintenance of mechanisms. It is important to note that in recent years a change of emphasis has taken in the field of international human rights. The initial focus was on setting standards as well as identifying and denouncing violations of human rights. Now there is an increasing interest in ensuring the effective implementation of human rights instruments. Monitoring of the obligations accepted by States and for implementing standard setting are many and varied. Therefore, instruments protecting equality, justice and morality within cyberspace increasingly contributes to a recipe for public administrative and operational services readily accessible by all.

The real test for monitoring of the Internet remains to be whether technology-ridden legislation can be implemented and made to work effectively. Codes of conduct should grow and be stimulated nationally first, with consumers and governments and legislature involved, bottom-up practices based on national concrete practices, i.e. national codes of conduct, must be favoured to a top-down approach.

12

UNESCO Virtual Forum on Infoethics

VF-INFOethics, an open worldwide electronic discussion forum carried out from October 1997 to April 1998, is presented in this chapter. This forum was organized as a follow-up to a recommendation made by the participants at the first INFOethics Congress held in Monaco from 10 to 12 March 1997. The forum was designed and managed by the Information Science Department of the University of Konstanz.

Objectives of the UNESCO Virtual Forum on INFOethics

VF-INFOethics is an open, world-wide electronic (virtual) discussion forum about information ethics.

The forum was proposed after the first UNESCO conference on Information Ethics, which took place in March 1997 in Monte Carlo. VF-INFOethics is not a substitute for meetings in a real-life environment — the advantage of face-to-face communication is too obvious and knowledge and experience with electronic forums is not yet wide-spread enough, at least not among UNESCO experts, who are normally not the typical Internet users (USA/Europe, male, highly-educated, 30 years old). But experimenting with electronic forums can provide UNESCO with knowledge about the potentials of the new medium and can contribute to a more extended word-wide awareness about the importance of information ethics in a globalizing information society. VF-INFOethics thus supports UNESCO's objective as a world-wide laboratory of ideas, in this case via a forum on information ethics, identifying ethical principles, guiding action, devising immaterial strategies and mobilizing political leaders in their resolve to implement them. As potentials or value-added effects of electronic communication forums the following deserve mention:

- Electronic communication forums allow exchange of information between people who are not likely to meet in real life.
- Electronic communication forums, organized according to hypertext principles, allow flexible navigation in heterogeneous information material and can thus develop into a platform of knowledge with respect to the topic of the forum.
- Electronic communication forums, in a Web-based technical environment are normally organized in an asynchronous mode (although synchronous chat techniques or tele-conferencing facilities are becoming more and more available for forum purposes as well). Asynchronous communication allows quasi real-time reactions to the forum's statements but also allows delayed reactions after a period of information gathering or, simply, of thinking.

- Electronic communication forums, compared with the high costs for real conferences with participants from all over the world, are a cheap technology once the technical equipment is available.
- Electronic communication forums, in particular when data-base supported, allow flexible adaptation to different users' needs/expectations, or to users' dialogue behaviour, and to different pre-established parameters such as access and editing rights.

Although the advantages of electronic forums are obvious, the hopes for VF-INFOethics were only moderately high because we could not expect that knowledge and experience with new electronic communication devices would be very advanced among UNESCO experts. This was all the more likely, given the fact that we tried to avoid an Anglo-saxon and Western-Europe dominated expertise and insisted instead on selecting people from all over the world. The particants were chosen on the basis of UNESCO expertise and recommendations from active members. Only these experts, altogether about 60, had the right to write, but the forum, as a WWW application, was open to the public for reading purposes.

The forum's main objective was to augment knowledge and public awareness on topics concerning information ethics and to provide UNESCO with recommendations for further action in the field of information ethics based on the world-wide electronic discussion among experts in the field.

In addition to statements from experts, additional information, for example references to pertinent literature on information ethics, to other web sites, to data bases, and to other discussion groups with a similar scope was provided by the central Constance monitoring group of VF-INFOethics. Additional links could be provided by all members of VF-INFOethics. VF-INFOethics has thus developed into an open forum, a platform, or a market place with numerous links to the world's knowledge on information ethics.

The INFOethics forum was carried out in two rounds. The first round lasted from October 97 until the end of the year 1998. The second round was opened for discussion as of Februar 20th 1998. At the end of round 2, UNESCO can be provided with recommendations for further action. It is very likely that the forum will continue to be an electronic floor for UNESCO-related discussions on INFOethics and will then be opened (also for writing purposes) to a broader UNESCO public or to the public in general. This, of course, will raise many new problems. In the near future, the forum will be used before, during and after the second UNESCO conference on INFOethics, which will take place in October 1998, again in Monte Carlo. The software, which was developed for VF-INFOethics and which is continously being improved, can be used for other UNESCO activities, in particular by national commissions for UNESCO or for educational purposes. At the moment, we are using the VF-INFOethics software for a virtually organized course on information ethics in the information science curriculum at the University of Konstanz, Germany.

Information ethics and the role of UNESCO

The forum was opened with a brief general statement about the concept of information ethics:

Information ethics, in general, is the study of commonly held values related to the belief in equality of access, justice and mutual respect arising from the development and application of new information and telecommunications technologies (e.g. the Internet).

Information ethics concerns many fields such as philosophy (ethics), anthropology/ethnology, linguistics, economics, law, sociology, political science, education, religion/theology, artificial intelligence, information and computer science. Information ethics covers both the private/individual and the public/institutional aspects of ethical problems, more and more on a global basis.

For many people, information ethics is likely to be considered as a substitute for traditional civic behavior in the advancing global information society. For UNESCO, information ethics is particularly related to science, education, culture, and civil society in general, both in developed and in developing countries.

The role of UNESCO in information ethics in general

The following questions were formulated with respect to the role of UNESCO in information ethics in general:

Considering UNESCO's role in the growing information society, information ethics in the understanding of this forum is particularly related to science, education, culture, art, society in general, both with respect to developed and to developing countries.

How can UNESCO promote understanding of information ethics issues and assist governments and other organizations in dealing with them? How can

UNESCO help in the harmonization of different ethical systems and in their co-existence in the new global information society? Is it UNESCO's mission to set up a universally accepted instrument of ethical behavior for information providers and users in the global information markets, especially in the developing information society? Should UNESCO develop an International Observatory on these issues?

The role of UNESCO: Information rich and poor

The following questions were formulated with respect to the role of UNESCO on the topic ,Information rich and information poor':

What can UNESCO do to prevent modern societies from being divided into the information elite and the information underprivileged? Is there a need and a chance for UNESCO to fill the widening "abstraction gap" between the dominant information rich and the information poor? Is UNESCO an appropriate advocate to defend the rights of the information underprivileged? What is the role of organizations such as UNESCO in overcoming the information and communication gap both within countries and between them?

With education being considered a major means to overcome the barriers between information rich and information poor - what can UNESCO do to help topics in information ethics be included in curricula at all levels of education?

Can UNESCO play a major role in programs designed to overcome the language barriers between people and nations? How can UNESCO protect the language rights of the non-English-speaking-world against economic interests in one-world-one-language markets?

When information competence is both the ability to access/use globally available information and the ability to produce information services - what can UNESCO do both to allow easy access to the global information resources and to move more passive (reading) societies into active (writing) societies?

What can UNESCO do to protect the rights of developing countries to represent their own way of thinking, of culture, science and economy in regional and global information networks and services?

The discussion on this topic was rather intensive. As a result of the discussion on the topic ,Information rich and information poor' the following recommendations were formulated.

- Bring net access to poor countries by putting existing resources to sensible use in order to promote the development of global and local information cultures and economies.
- Support the development of a World Information Ethos.
- Support concrete projects in information poor countries in order to create country-specific information centres.
- Public awareness on these matters through virtual forums, publications, and conferences should be promoted.
- Provide permanent, specific, and detailed knowledge of existing information activities in information poor countries.

- UNESCO should promote the rights of non-English-speaking-countries and their economic interests.
- UNESCO should promote topics in information ethics to be included in curricula at all levels.
- Promotion activities through international organizations should be based on grassroots efforts as well as on a decentralized and well coordinated basis.

The role of UNESCO: public and/or private good

The following questions were formulated with respect to the role of UNESCO on the topic Information as a public and/or a private good:

What can UNESCO do to help the development of public/private structures as an appropriate balance between economic and social interests? What can UNESCO do to achieve and finance the provision of information falling in the public domain to all members of the societies in all countries? What can UNESCO do to provide open access to the world public knowledge heritage? What can UNESCO do to develop a world-wide awareness for the importance of information and communication technologies and systems for all societies and for the balance between them?

As the result of the discussion on the topic ,Information as a public and/or private good' the following summary was formulated.

"Information as a public and/or a private good" stimulated some discussion about the status of information in modern societies. Some concern was expressed about the negative effects of modern information structures (virtualization) on the job market. The participants did not see any realistic alternative economic model by which the shortcomings of the neo-liberalism approach could be overcome. It was suggested that cooperatives may play a major role in the usage of information as a common good. UNESCO should not get involved in general abstract discussions about a new world order. Instead UNESCO should concentrate on feasible projects such as supporting efforts for the digitization of public information (as the world people's heritage) as a counterweight to the power of the market, where information is considered a commodity only.

The role of copyright should be reconsidered as well in order to define a new generally accepted fair use of information. By encouraging free access to the world's public knowledge (the people's own heritage) UNESCO can contribute to establishing a counterweight to the power of the market, where information is considered a commodity to be paid for. UNESCO should use a set amount of funds to support the digitization of public material (e.g. to finance portable scanners). The role of copyright (so far mainly used to enforce market rights) should be reconsidered. Particularly, the rights of users to access public materials should be balanced against the predominantly private exploitation of information. Preservation and transmission of information was considered as among the ethical responsibilities of the present for future generations.

The role of UNESCO: Trust, ownership, and validity of information in cyberspace

The following questions were formulated with respect to

the role of UNESCO on the topic ,Trust, ownership, and validity of information in cyberspace':

What can be done by UNESCO in order to establish an ethics instrument for information/content providers by which they may be obliged to care for trustworthy, approved, or true information? Which is the main role of UNESCO in the new property right debate, for example on digital objects? What can UNESCO do to establish a new "fair use" and/or "copyleft" of information which establishes a compromise between the rights of the holders and the interests of society to have free access to information?

Can UNESCO play an active role in establishing trust in information services and electronic markets, in particular when sensitive subjects are involved, such as medicine, law, or political information? Is UNESCO an appropriate and world-wide accepted institution to develop, maintain, and survey generally accepted quality criteria for the reliability and authenticity of information services? What is the role of UNESCO in establishing trust in machine intelligence and services such as intelligent agents or in keeping it under public control?

There was an innovative and provocative proposal to rethink the role of copyright: It doesn't make any sense for authors who already get paid by public institutions to receive additional copyright income. Giving up copyright income could break the circle of high prices and lack of access, at least in scientific environments. Access to the world's knowledge should have higher priority than supporting commercial interest in information commodities. A different answer may be required with respect to entertainment and literature.

On the other hand it was not considered realistic that authors would voluntarily give up commercial rights. Therefore it is not sufficient to change our attitude towards ownership and profit. A solution could be for publishing companies to pay a certain percentage of the author's income to the public, which is explicitly designed for supporting the construction of a powerful and royalty-free world wide public domain of information. This idea of sharing profits from knowledge products can be extended to all organizations which produce value-adding information/knowledge products originally based on publicly produced and financed primary/raw information for the market.

UNESCO is not either WIPO or WTO (although the protection of authors/publishers' rights cannot be ignored, it is not the main concern for UNESCO). Instead UNESCO must bring its own added value to the debate on intellectual property rights, and this means to promote the free flow of ideas by word and image, to give fresh impulse to popular education, and to support all means for the diffusion of knowledge. All scientific articles produced by public universities or public laboratories could be made freely available on the servers of these institutions.

UNESCO should take the lead in a world wide movement to promote this public domain information, and present innovative ideas to ensure distribution and free access to it. In particular with respect to developing countries, economic barriers created by a purely market oriented approach towards knowledge and information need to be overcome. UNESCO should use all its prestige to convince governments and institutions involved in the information/knowledge industry all over the world that they should share profits from knowledge products (especially those which are originally based on publicly produced and financed primary/raw information) with public institutions. These institutions then can produce value-added free-access information for those who cannot afford to pay for it.

The role of UNESCO: Privacy, confidentiality, security, hate, violence in the Internet

The following questions were formulated with respect to the role of UNESCO on the topic ,Privacy, confidentiality, security, hate, violence in the Internet':

What are appropriate measures for UNESCO in order to diminish the amount of violence and hate in the Internet? Is UNESCO the appropriate organization for developing a world-wide code for information privacy? Is such a code desirable or possible? What are appropriate control structures if such a privacy/confidentiality code were ever to be agreed on? What can UNESCO do to encourage and establish the free flow of information in the traditional and new media

Although the concept of information ethics was a topic of discussion in itself and was permanently referredto, there was no formal agreement about this concept besides general remarks such as that information ethics deals with principles of equality, justice and mutual respect under the conditions of a global information society.

Global networks and electronic market places and information services (in the Internet and other prorietary networks) are the environment and the only means in which and through which information ethics develops.

One can doubt whether there is a need (or a possibility) for something like information ethics (or science ethics or market ethics) in addition to ethics in general. The principles of ethics in general — if any — would also be valid for information ethics in particular. The forum's participants were particularly careful in simply transferring western ideas to a global information world and were also very concerned that the unification influence of the global Internet can lead to an unwanted dominant general and ethical culture. This is clearly to be seen on (ethical) topics such as property right, violence in the media, information access and information equity, individual freedom of information, where Western philosophical, political, and economic traditions dominate.

Information ethics is not a matter of abstract academic (philosophical) discussion and cannot result in a new (single) world order of information behaviour, but can be a permanent world-wide process of exchange of positions between people who are involved in structuring the new information world. The global information society is thus a platform for information ethics and the result of the discussion cannot be a single world information ethics but the development of an ethos that makes the public aware and sensitive of the need to take a responsible and not only merely economically determined approach towards information, its production, distribution and usage.

This is the major information ethic topic in the information society. The topic is in its global character comparable to ecological questions and should thus be treated on the same level of political decision-making and public disussion. There is a real need for an international information agenda. What VF-INFOethics thus recommends is the development of a world-wide public responsibilty for information equity (an information ethos) by establishing an institutionalized dialog on information policy issues at a world level, 'some authors hold that a new UN/UNESCO information agency would be an approriate institutional means - and by supporting an open world forum (or many interlinked forums) on information ethics, using the electronic medium and other media as well.

Both an institutionalized and a communicative approach will create global (and local!) information policies and information cultures. This means that one should give up the ideal of a rational, clean and transparent ethical world information order, and see the multi-cultural reality not as a threat but as an opportunity.

The continuing globalization of all aspects of the production, distribution and usage of information is the central challenge for information ethics. The production of information is based on the need for information and refers to its content and quality. The distribution of information raises the question of information ownership and depends on the information resources in which information is represented and on the design and management of information market places where information can be accessed and exchanged.

The usage of information is mainly a question of competence and money — being informationally educated in order to profit from the information resources and being able to pay for the costs of information usage. This is a (political) question of information equity or inequity or how to overcome information gaps.

Considering the importance of the global information society, it has turned out that the participants were mainly concerned about the growing gap between those who are able and willing to take advantage of modern information and communication technology and those who are not. The problem of information gaps cannot be restricted to the difference between developed and developing countries but is a problem in all societies, whatever their technological status. If access to information and the possibility to actively take part in the exchange of knowledge (to have the right to read and write in open information environments) is the necessary basis for all activities in our public and private life, then it is UNESCO's responsibility to support all activities which aim at establishing an information balance in the information society.

A society is information-balanced when information gaps can be overcome. Therefore a consideration of information equity seems to be at the center of all ethical discussion. This is not a technological problem. It cannot be solved by providing everyone in the world with a computer and telecommunication equipment (although the importance of such a programme — to provide in principle everyone with the technological basis needed — should not be underestimated), but by solving the information problem.

The forum's participants agreed that only a free market can develop powerful information market places, information systems and information goods but that there is a need for international organizations such as UNESCO and for other nation-wide activities to solve the global problem of information inequity. Overcoming information inequity does not necessarily mean that global information can be accessed from everywhere by everyone (and at no cost). The creation of content in an appropriate environment and the exchange of information among those whc need it (for instance, the south communicating with the south and not being restricted to access of information from the north, as is the case today) is increasingly important. What seems to be a paradox in a global information environment, namely the demand to create and use regionally pertinent information, is actually a necessity and a requirement for information use.

The emphasis on information production, distribution and usage topics from an ethical point of view raises many questions and generates many sub-topics, such as the following ones:

- Given the fact that information is cost-intensive to produce and thus demands a economic basis — who/which institution and which level will be responsible for granting access to appropriate information for the use of local actors'
- How can a basic information supply be defined and guaranteed?
- Which models are available to find a fair compromise between market interests in getting information cost investment returned with a reasonable profit and public interest in giving everyone the chance to lead their private and public life on an information-secure basis?
- Which are appropriate models for such information compromises on a super-national level (overcoming gaps between information rich and information poor countries), on a national level (gaps within an

information society), and on an individual level (gaps in information competence and education)?

As is often the case in communication-intensive matters, VF-INFOethics has raised more questions than it has answered. The only definite answer is that the discussion on information ethics needs to be continued, at all levels, within and outside UNESCO and using all available media, the electronic forum included.

How can you improve the success rate of e-government projects? By turning to prototyping; a technique increasingly on the e-government agenda. Prototyping - the creation of a small, live working model of a technology project ahead of full-scale development - is particularly suitable for e-government projects, where public money is at stake and efficiency is paramount. Technological changes have made prototyping quicker and easier. Benefits are readily apparent in creating a working model of e-government that users can see, comment on and have revised.

The physical presence of the model e-government system enables stakeholders to express requirements or objectives they would otherwise find hard to state. Such requirements may be quite general (e.g. about the overall objectives sought from the e-government application) or may be quite specific (e.g. a comment on the nature of the system interface). The presence of a system helps focus stakeholders' attention, envisage what they need from e-government, and point out what they do not like.

There are different kinds of prototyping, and one kind may suit a particular situation more than another. For example disposable prototyping builds a very small-scale model very early on that is not intended to be kept; whereas 'incremental prototyping' works gradually towards the final system. But whichever kind is used, prototyping means that:

- — the final e-government application is more likely to match stakeholder objectives;
- — stakeholders are more realistic in what they expect from the final system;
- — the final system may be produced more quickly;
- — major problems are spotted earlier, and can therefore be addressed at lower cost.

There may also be additional benefits. New York State's Office for the Aging introduced e-government to support coordinated delivery of client services. Through use of prototyping, they found not just application improvements but also greater levels of interest and commitment from management. As the Center for Technology in Government reports, "The prototyping method produced positive results. ... early demonstrations of the system created an enthusiastic response among local governments and generated positive interest in the system among the user community".

Systems development methodologies that incorporate prototyping have been around for many years. For example, prototyping has been successfully incorporated into the Dynamic Systems Development Method. This provides a standard, non-proprietary approach to systems development that combines both rapid and joint application development methods.

Such combinations of prototyping and active participation can be particularly effective for e-government projects. The Royal Netherlands Air Force, for example, used both techniques through a management game involving the simulation of a 'whole-organisation' digital system for a planned air base. Not only did this create a shared vision for change among participants, it also facilitated discussion of key issues, and created a sense of unity between those involved. As a result, this has been recommended as a standard approach to e-government projects.

As with any project management technique, prototyping of e-government projects can have its drawbacks. Time pressures may force premature acceptance of the prototype before all requirements are fully analysed, before non-technical components of the system are designed, or before the system is properly tested and documented. Prototyping may encourage corners to be cut, yet it does not substitute for techniques to create consensus or for good communications between IT staff and users.

Nevertheless, prototyping is increasingly used in e-government and will increasingly be seen as a critical success factor in the development process.

Bibliography

"Artificial Intelligence: The Second Computer Age Begins", *Business Week*, March 8, 1982.

Bluestone Barry and Bennett Harisn, *The Deindustrialisation of America: Plant Closure, Community Abandonment and the Dismantling of Basic Industry*, Basic Books, New York, 1982.

Burns, T. and Stalker, G. *The Management of Innovation* (2nd edn.). Tavistock, 1968.

Butler, Gathorne. *Organisation and Management*, Prentice Hall, 1986.

Brendan P. Kehoe, Zen and the Art of the Internet: A Beginner's Guide. 2nd ed., Englewood Cliffs, NJ: Prentice Hall, 1993.

Computer-Based National Information Systems: Technology and Public Policy Issues Office of Technology Assessment, US Congress, Washington, DC, 1981.

Daniel, Evelyn, 'Information resources and organisational structure', *Journal of the American Society for Information Science*, 1983.

"Electronic Money; So Much for the Cashless Society", The Economist, November 26, 1994 (Special edition).

Gold Bela, "CAM Sets New Rules for Production", *Harvard Business Review*, November-December 1983.

Hafner Katie, Where Wizards Stay Up at Night: The Story Behind the Creation of the Internet New York: Simon and Schuster, 1996.

Information Superhighway: Issues Affecting Development" (GAO/RECD-94-22285), September 30, 1994.

"Interactive Advertising in an Online World", Information Week, October 3, 1994.

Leonard-Barton; Dorothy and Kraus, William 'Implementing new technology', *Harvard Business Review*, Nov./Dec. 1985.

Lloyd Andrew, "Europe Examines Electronic Democracy", New Scientist, June 2, 1983. On Council of Europe report, *New Possibilities for Democratic Participation Resulting From Information and Communication Technology*, Brussels, 1983.

Medvinsky Gennady and B. Clifford Neuman, "NetCash: A Design for Practical Electronic Currency on the Internet", Proceedings of the first ACM conference on Computer and Communication Security, November 1993.

Mandeville Thomas, "The Spatial Effects of Information Technology", *Futures*, February 1983. A review of the literature on possible urban/regional problems.

Request for Comments: 1192, "Commercialisation of the Internet", B. Kahin, Ed., November 1990, Harvard University.

"The Future of Electronic Commerce Explored at EM 2000", SIMBA Information Inc's Electronic Marketplace 2000 trade show, Electronic Marketplace Reports, March 15, 1994.

Index